Returning to Happiness…
****
Overcoming Depression with Body, Mind, and Spirit

by Patricia Gaviria

Moving Energies

© PATRICIA GAVIRIA
© MOVIENDO ENERGÍAS / MOVING ENERGIES

"Returning to Happiness… Overcoming Depression with Body, Mind, and Spirit"

Print Third Edition 2022
ISBN: 978-0-9972744-4-8
Library of Congress Control Number: 2019901396
Publisher: Moving Energies / Moviendo Energías
Wellington, Florida – United States of America
movingenergies@live.com

Print First Edition 2015
ISBN: 978-0-9910997-6-4
This work is a translation of the original Spanish title:
"Volver a Ser Feliz… Venciendo la Depresión con el Cuerpo, la Mente y el Espíritu"   Also available in Portuguese.

Translated into English by *Patricia Gaviria* as her second language.
Design of Cover, Interior, and Graphics: *Patricia Gaviria.*

NOTES TO READER:
 - The subject presented in this book is not a Medical or Psychological approach; rather it is a subjective conceptualization based on the author's personal experience. Any professional treatment or medications used by the reader should not be suspended. The author and publisher do not take responsibility for any action taken by the reader after reading the content of this work.
- Some material from Patricia Gaviria books is transcribed one in other. She intends to set different scenarios for the same text, giving the reader a new perspective and mayor comprehension of the subject.   - The content references The Urantia Book, 2nd Spanish edition, published by The Urantia Foundation in 1996.

© The Urantia Foundation - all rights reserved - 533 Diversey Parkway, Chicago, Illinois 60614, USA; +1 (773) 525-3319   www.urantia.org
The opinions expressed in this book are exclusive of the author and do not necessarily represent the opinions of Urantia Foundation or its members.

This book is dedicated to those who one day, in their desperation and unfruitful search for inner peace and relief... took the unfortunate step to end their own lives.

CONTENT

Dear Reader
****

Sometimes when looking around, it feels like nothing makes sense. Your emotions are perceived strange. Life appears complicated because you are out of energy or capacity to face problems that strike daily, and on many occasions, the desire to continue living tends to vanish.

You hold the sensation of having fallen unexpectedly into a pond of cloudy waters, where you were thrown by circumstances very difficult to understand. Your arms and legs shake with vigor and your body weight pulls you towards the bottom of the water. The fear of being airless incapacitates you from coordinating corporal movements, and instead of finding even one light to guide the way to the surface where you can breathe, you get completely exhausted and hopeless.

In the middle of the confusion, you think you are alone, and although wishing to be afloat, you end up drowning in the depths of an unknown environment.

But strangely, on some occasions, a great force surrounds and carries you to enjoy the scene unfolding above the turbulent and abysmal torrent. It seems like as soon as you reach the open space and take a profound inhalation, your eyes glimpse a different world. There is light, breeze, sounds, and colors. Your emotions rise, the anguish dissipates, and staying alive no longer requires effort. The atmosphere is now warm and familiar, convincing yourself that this is the place where truly you belong.

And even if once again you feel debilitated, allowing the treacherous currents to drag you into darkness and silence where slow asphyxia suspends existence, be sure that this invisible and powerful hand will carry you to solid land forever.

Just hold onto the security that it will be so someday. Moreover, that day… could be today!

Introduction
****

Today, I remember my husband's astonished expression while hanging up the phone, and his sad glance when sharing with me the just received news: "Felipe, our dear friend, took his own life."

How could this be?

If less than a year earlier, another of our "dear friends" had made the same decision.

How could this be?

If they were friendly, young, healthy, and successful fellows, with small children and beautiful families; if not long ago, we all shared good moments and everything seemed to be fine.

How could this be?

The answer in both cases was the same: "They were depressed."

At that moment, I decided to tell my story. I promised God and myself that, somehow, I would narrate the process that allowed me to take a different path from the one chosen by my forever remembered friends… would introduce the *internal voice* that gave me strength to stay afloat during times of despair and distress… would share the hope of living life with courage, tranquility, and joy.

By writing this book, perhaps, I could touch the hearts of people who are immersed in difficult stages of Depression. Perhaps, my words would be the inspiration for them to make some changes. Perhaps, I might offer a clue, which guides them toward a complete personal transformation.

It contains numerous elements: real memories of particular and even unusual events that describe the depressive condition from which I suffered over the course of many years; philosophical analyses that lead to an understanding of human nature; new and refreshing concepts explaining the causes of depressive states, regarding each one of the primary energy currents that compose the self (body, mind, and spirit) and the effects that are generated when they vibrate at low frequency levels. In addition, I provide practical advice in the use of natural and innate tools that balance the physical, mental, and emotional aspects of life.

I want to clarify that this approach is not informed by fields such as Medicine, Psychiatry, or Psychology, nor under any circumstance, it is meant to interfere with medical treatments the reader may be in. Rather, it is based entirely on my personal experience and a subjective theoretical conceptualization, with the intention to offer an alternative for those who are constantly searching for a way to feel better and are ready to take practical, natural, and permanent measures.

To read "Returning to Happiness..." is a great adventure that I invite to take. And I congratulate those who confront the challenge because I am convinced that, like me, they will realize the human being true essence is to be well, and overcoming Depression is much easier than they ever imagined.

Finally, I must thank my divine "Thought Adjuster" that has been the architect of my existence. To my parents, for their love and unconditional support. To my husband and children, for being fundamental components of my progress. To all my "life-pals" whom, with an open heart, have accepted my help and teachings to make transformational changes in their lives. And to many others that collaborated making this work a reality...

which I have faith, will inspire millions!

Patricia Gaviria

FIRST PART

I will never forget the unpleasant sensation I had when entering the shady office of that eccentric looking Psychiatrist, who was waiting for me on the other side of his desk.

When he asked: "What is happening to you?" My being gave a great sigh and kept silent. How to answer the question had been with me for so many years and yet had no explanation?

How can I explain, "What is happening to me?" - I thought. "Where should I begin? How do I bring to light the things living inside me, which I never had the courage to show, even to closest people? How long would it take to expose the stormy feelings in my heart and the thoughts tormenting my mind?"

I had to collect each piece of the puzzle of my life and position them, one by one, back into place. Perhaps it would be the only way to answer so complex question!

I
Magical Childhood

It is important to say that my first years of life were pleasant. I was born into a wonderful family (my parents and two brothers) in which love, tenderness, cordiality, and union were fundamental parts of our education. In addition, I grew up in a small city known for its friendly and open people, who offered me gratifying moments that will be in my memory forever.

I was a sociable, creative, cheerful, curious, and active girl. I loved music, art, dance, and, most of all, was passionate about learning. Regardless of the subject, my mind had thousands of questions and I tried to find answers no matter what; which led me to be a good student and always listening attentively to people who had something to teach.

While facing new matters, I handled insecurities with beautiful childish innocence. Like the fear experienced when I thought the wool blanket, placed on the big armchair in front of my bed, was a scary monster watching me during the night.

Nothing prevented me from being open or expressing my feelings frankly to those around me.

This allowed me to have a good connection with my family, made many friends, and even captivated some young boys' hearts who offered me a "just words" relationship because they were too shy to take my hand.

I always had what I needed. I was fortuned to travel around the world and face enriching experiences, which combined with my tropical, jovial, and full of contrasts -sometimes extremes- Latin culture, added a particular life point of view to my personality.

When I think about my childhood, many pleasant memories fulfill me. However, there is something always catches my attention... something that from a very early age became part of my conduct, and it is a common behavior to most children regardless race, gender, or nationality.

While playing alone, I would naturally and instinctively create a *monologue* in which I asked questions and also answered them. Usually, it seemed like I was talking to another person; making many adults curious and ready to interrogate: "Who are you talking to?"
But, to be honest, I don't remember my response!

What I sure do remember is this self-communication was like a game. A game that, little by little, not only became part of my daily life, but would also be a key element in my coming years of development...

Reflections of My Experience...

During my childhood I experienced the wonderful sensation of freedom; the freedom to be what I wanted to be.

I learned that all children are born with innate and valuable tools necessary for proper development, and the correct use of those tools allows them to perceive an atmosphere that can be described as "magical."

From a young age, kids are ready for adventures with spirit and joy. Constantly, they explore their senses: listening, hearing, touching, smelling, and tasting everything that is new and draws their attention. Their curiosity is insatiable and their capacity to enjoy the simple and natural is enviable.

They know, for sure, they are an integral part of the environment.

Loving to be in action, they instinctively move in a rhythmical and recreational way. Music, imagination, humor, and self-expression (expressed through games, dances, or any pirouette their elastic bodies can handle) will make them feel full of energy and joviality.

Their goal is to always find something that makes them laugh... something that gives them thrill.

They are honest with themselves and others, having no fear of judgment; sharing with playmates of different ages, races, cultures, or languages without prejudices. They don't act with the intention to please or to force others to do exactly as they do; expressing without lies or masquerades, like when innocently they say on the phone: "My mother just told me she is not here."

They simply are, and let the world simply be.

They offer love and tenderness unconditionally; waiting for nothing in return and harbor no resentment against those who don't express the same sentiments. They are affectionate by nature, knowing love expressions stimulate the spirit.

They give for the pleasure of giving and not for the pleasure of receiving.

They hold the incredible ability of going step by step, moment by moment; enjoying everything that arrives, without worrying what will come later. When children want something, they simply go for it, free from anguish and fear. And when they have a dream, they know in fact life will give it to them, never questioning how.

Believing is not up for discussion.

Magical, yes, *magical* is the world's view kids have through their open minds and young hearts; allowing the universal wisdom guide and make them feel the true essence of existence.

"During my childhood, I learned the little ones have the key to being happy and free… to being what they want, and what they must be."

II
Difficult Awakening

Life was normal and pleasant until I reached the first stages of adolescence -around twelve years of age- when, little by little, everything began to change.

As new experiences were faced, I left the "enchanted" world of my childhood and enter a different one, for which I was unprepared. My conscience started to realize I was an independent piece in the big social system, with unique thoughts and unique feelings. But, unfortunately, yet lost in who I really was, I couldn't get my own concepts about life or personal tastes that determined my way to dress, to speak, to act, to live.

The ability of early years to openly express myself was disappearing gradually, and I ended up going around with introversion and shyness. A feeling of insecurity, almost fear, overtook me when I had to show others the new emerging individual who "I" barely knew. In addition, I assumed that everybody else understood the whole reason of life, perfectly confident in their desires and thoughts. Therefore, my self-confidence began to appear only when provided by somebody else.

Simple decisions, such as whether to drink soda, water, or juice… whether to wear the white or the blue dress… or whether to go to one place or another, created a huge emotional storm. If someone asked me a direct question, waiting for a specific answer, my heart would beat forcefully and my hands would dampen with the sweat produced by nervousness. My mind would be blocked and my voice would be mute.

I began, then, to walk constantly with my head facing down, evading people's glances; and my only relief was to find lost things on the ground. I also recall when boarding the school bus, saying "hello" to the driver in a whispered voice, and looking just with the corner of my eye for the first seat available; wishing not to be seen or talked to… wishing to disappear!

In class, I didn't dare raise my hand when I had a question or comment, because I was afraid of being judged by others for doing or saying something incorrect; for not fitting into the society I had been a part of in past days.

My unstable personality generated contradictory ideas and emotions because I felt incapable of fitting into the social structure or managing my own convictions, firmness, and independence. This is how I began isolating myself in a world of very few participants.

But "we never know when life is reserving us a surprise." The practice I had as a young girl of speaking to myself began to take an unexpected course. No longer were my own thoughts and words, but a second *voice* entered to be part of the conversation.

It was not a real voice because it was soundless; rather, there were vibrations placed in my brain, like if someone else was writing or typing information into it. These exchanges seemed a pleasant chat, during which I exposed my concepts about different subjects and received new ideas that should be processed and interpreted.

Was it the voice of my conscience? Tricks of my own mind? Just intuition? Or, perhaps, some special spiritual being who was next to me?   I didn't know!

Fortunately, I was never scared. The process occurred instinctively and naturally, as I was younger. It was such a comfortable sensation of peace and joy. Every night, lying on my bed, I anxiously hoped to communicate with this supposed *voice* that offered me hours of conversation; sharing my obstinate obsession to analyze life, question everything, and search for true answers.

As a result of these dialogues, I took a very different perspective about people's behavior and way of thinking, the morality and religion I was raised with, the role of women in society, the real meaning of creation, and many other aspects that worried me. Questioning why suffering, wickedness, and inequality exist in our world or why so many good people like me couldn't manage to find peace, calm, and a state of complete realization.

Hundreds of the new concepts I was acquiring were very logical to me. Nevertheless, sometimes, they seemed so different and opposite from those expressed by the traditions of my developing third-world country's culture. I felt like I belonged to another world, far away from the one in which I was born.

With this special energy surrounding me, I was convinced something powerful, wise, and supreme surely exists... something far, but simultaneously near... something unknown, but at the same time familiar... something that speaks, but keeps silent... something to which I couldn't give a name at the moment, but, unquestionably, was a real part of me.

Day after day, this *voice* filled me with relief, and somehow became my companion and confidante. However, I would still be very far from reaching an emotional tranquility and full understanding of what was really happening...

Reflections of My Experience...

In those early years of my adolescence, I understood that during our growth, natural and innate factors indispensable for a life full of well-being are frequently blocked.

Many, and sometimes most, of the tools children are born with are disrupted by unsuitable systems imposed by society. While they are exposed to concepts and habits opposite of their essence, their normal behavior begins to change. Little by little, joy disappears; there is no more space for imagination, self-knowledge, or self-expression; the meaning of existence gets distorted; and, especially, making contact with those universal forces that provide power and wisdom within us is no longer easy.

The reason lies in devastating events occurred thousands and thousands of years ago. Humanity's way of thinking, acting, and feeling were affected, which generated an inaccurate and unstable base for the creation of future social, educational, and religious structures.

True and real aspects were mixed with false and unrealistic ones; creating great confusion that would interrupt our original connection to the rest of the universe. And, even if the world continued its evolution for centuries, overwhelming loads were brought to the present generations.

Today we are submerged in cultures with conditions far from those human beings should be exposed. Children are forced to adopt abnormal identities in order to fit in, they lose the knowledge of how to interact correctly with others and with *Mother Nature*, and the internal communication with the divine energy disappears almost completely. So it is not a surprise we continue facing facts that deteriorate our species, injustices hard to understand, genetic transformations and diseases that shouldn't be part of our being, and conditions that generate disturbing emotions. Sometimes, leading us to wonder how the mighty God allows all this to happen.

But, paying attention, we may realize the natural instincts we were born with always stay latent inside us. Somehow, a bond with the force that preserves our original heritage still exists. And although it is beyond our knowledge to understand exactly what it is or who it is, we have to be convinced this omnipotent energy is available for our evolution, or is at least ready for those who want to return to it.

Thus, for the young people who keep the essence of their origins and avoid adverse circumstances, life will unfold properly. Conversely, the ones forced to follow traditions that don't evolve, and learn concepts that go against their natural disposition, will develop troubled and unstable personalities.

Each generation comes filled with updated information from the previous one; and even if this is a key element for social progress, it is why many children's behaviors appear illogical to their parents.

Traditions are fundamental aspects of life; however, these should never obstruct the power that kids bring with their new and advanced ways of thinking and acting. Adults will always have the necessary experience for teaching, but they should never underestimate the universe's supreme knowledge, which leaves its trace on the beings that are born every day.

"In the beginning of my adolescence I understood that when kids are forced to change their original essence, they will have a hard time facing teenage years and it will be almost impossible to build a good adulthood. Even so, the relationship with the great universal energy may be suspended, but, luckily, can never be ended."

III
Confusing Reality

In the following years, almost all the ideas I acquired through the conversations, seemed polar opposite from those the society had; so, unfortunately, anguish, insecurity, and a feeling of disorientation grew within me.

I began to perceive the world's indifference towards problems, such as misery, war, lack of education, physical and mental health deficiencies, and much more. My logic was overwhelmed when I saw children thrown in the street with no food, no home, no love, no life; how disrespect, violence, and death were interlaced in daily routine. And my heart cracked when the faces of good and worthy people had pronounced traces of resentment as a result of the constant fight against a system that denied them even one of the basic human rights: to learn how to sign their own names.

I noticed the beautiful and special essence of *women* was repressed by a patriarchal society; where their freedom to act, learn, and achieve were denied, so they were forced to appear and involuntarily be the inferior gender. However, I knew if women could somehow recover their true values and innate strength, they would conquer and change the destiny of future female generations.

I recall carefully listening to the religious sermon every Sunday in church. Many things can be rescued from these gatherings, but, in general, most of my questions didn't have logical answers and other times I couldn't even get explanations.

I refused to accept the idea that the human race was created to suffer. That we learn and grow through pain and hurtful experiences; that we are paying for the guilt of some "original sin" committed long ago, and are condemned to carry a "cross" for the rest of our days if we don't feel remorse for something incomprehensible. Or that God is very far away, reached only by saints, and those who do not approach that saintliness will sink into dark worlds of punishment and more agony.

I didn't think we are *sinners* as religion wants to teach us. Rather, I saw us as *apprentices* beginning a long journey to acquire a higher conscience, and this status does not convert us into rejected beings that are punished by the universe.

I felt so strange and was incapable of sharing my feelings with anybody. I felt confident of my thoughts but unconfident of my emotions.

Being sure, we all have the right to find answers for our doubts, and because my religion did not manage to give me the expected support, I decided to walk different roads.

I embraced the study of the most influential religions preached around the world, but even so, none appeared to calm my restlessness. Then I explored Metaphysics, Spiritism, and Esoterism; with activities like tarot, hand and tobacco reading, games to contact spirits, astral projections, and past-life regressions, among others. Unfortunately, the hundreds of new concepts such as karma, reincarnation, possession, or clairvoyance were not logical enough to clarify my confusion; producing a more intense mental storm and daze.

A difficult stage had begun!

My heart became aware about worldwide problems, yet I felt incapable of doing something to change it. An inner *voice* was accommodating my thoughts, but never answered questions as: Who or what was it? Where did it come from? Why if it was part of my brain, at the same time, it didn't sense like mine? And, even though my search continued with dedication, fear prevented me from asking these questions openly because I didn't want to be called "crazy."

Frequent strong headaches, accompanied by vomiting, started to paralyze me for days. I consumed many pills to alleviate the pain; however, the normal doses quickly were ineffective, pushing me to reach for stronger medicines that harmed my body in other ways.

And if this wasn't enough, I had to confront new situations in the romantic side of life while discovering *love*. What it is for most people a pleasant and enriching stage became a nightmare for me.

In front of the mirror I observed a barely developed girl, too skinny, with pale broken-out skin, and a used-broom look like hair; displaying cero attractiveness for the opposite sex. All my school years were spent at exclusively women institutions; therefore, a close encounter with an *extraterrestrial being* would have been simpler than communicating with a boy. I was the "Ugly Duckling" who nobody wanted to ask for dancing at parties or to keep a conversation for more than half minute.

My self-judgment turned into rejection and all this confusion redirected the course of my great searching.

Now, a desire, almost obsession, appeared in the form of finding *"Prince Charming"* who would give me happiness forever, as shown in the most popular fairytales: Snow White and Cinderella. I thought if I could get the attention of a protective gentleman, magically the worry, shyness, and anxiety would vanish. I was convinced my sadness was caused by not having *somebody* to show me how to enjoy life, motivate me, tell me I was worthy and intelligent; and persuade me that, yes, I belonged to the normal world.

But the more distressed I became about finding my rescuer, the faster the possibilities disappeared. Moreover, I understand now, I would never have been able to find him.

At the end of this stage, I faced many emotional shocks, and one of the most critical and delicate periods of my journey was about to begin…

Reflections of My Experience...

During these years of my development, I comprehended that when lacking self-knowledge and self-esteem, we experience paralyzing and destructive conditions.

Millions and millions of individuals go invisible while facing society, incapable of expressing or acting freely. And most of the time, with displeasure, they end up doing what others want and playing the games imposed by social structures.

When resigning to construct our own personality and security, we sink into uncertain emotions that leave our life control in the hands of someone or something else. We accept inappropriate behaviors, provided that we don't feel rejected or despised... provided that somebody wants and needs us... provided that we may fit in the system. And if we do not obtain an unconditional acceptance from others, or at least their compassion, we collapse and think we are drowning.

We are easily convinced that in order to have a space in the normal world we must be good-looking, have degrees, important positions, and wealth; that we have value just when fulfilling the requirements determined by a culture that has lost the authentic recognition deserved by all children of the universe.

So, despair and envy grow as we feel threatened by people who appear more intelligent, attractive or prosperous than us; creating an obsession with finding the perfect love, the perfect job, or maybe the perfect body that will satisfy this great space overwhelming our soul.

When our identity is shadowed, we build a life full of fear. Fear of being unloved, having less, abandoning yearnings and dreams; frightened of the future, of the death.

We learn to be scared and we get used to it!

It is necessary to be careful when searching for our own value and not to fall into an "egocentric" mindset. With this condition of learned behaviors we look very self-secure, but in reality there is an internal emptiness that has to be filled; so we try to control others by imposing our thoughts at all costs, wanting always to be right, emphasizing everybody else's weaknesses, and depending on constant praise.

This egocentricity is a distorted self-esteem, and it doesn't even come close of being true self-knowledge.

But it seems like the *internal voice* is a fundamental component in discovering our personality… it seems like this "whisper" opens the conscience not only to an outer world, but also to an inner one… it seems like she knows more about us than we do… it seems like she has a simultaneous individual and collective wisdom that teaches our true nature.

This is why the less we understand who she is, the less we understand about ourselves. And the more difficult the connection with her, the more complicated it is to have clarity of our individual identity and existence.

"During this period of my life, I visualized that self-knowledge and self-esteem are some of the most difficult aspects to acquire. But, maybe, the comprehension of what this *mysterious mental voice* is, or how she works in every person, could be the direct key to staying connected with our original essence."

IV
Limit of
My Reality

When I was about fifteen, many aspects began to extinguish the hope of finding the magical key would take me out of this emotional hollow into which I had fallen.

I was living in a world that nobody seemed to perceive, and, definitively, I didn't want them to perceive. In general, my behavior looked normal, but there was a constant internal battle where I fought not to feel what I felt... not to think what I thought... not to wish what I wished.

My family offered me a pleasant environment, but in my inner self, there was just conflict. I wanted to scream and tell all of my loved ones how my life was; however, I thought they already had enough difficulties to also carry with my confusions and sorrows. I assumed this was a situation that could only be solved by me.

I envied people who maintained their joy when facing serious problems, considering how difficult was for me to be happy. Every inconvenience, regardless of how small it was, intensified the anguish and affected my ability to make decisions.

My main emotion was fear and any smile drawn on my face was faked.

When looking towards the future, my mind became cloudy and unable to identify what could happen next. There were no dreams, passions, or goals to reach. And even with great effort to succeed, I felt like I was completely incompetent and would always fail.

Being socially active and doing the things I enjoyed as a little girl became much more difficult. The distress increased. I didn't want to go anywhere or speak to anyone. When I was surrounded by a lot of people, my heart rate accelerated and my breathing almost interrupted; this is why restrooms became a safe zone when I wanted to evade this situation, and luckily they are available everywhere.

I started experiencing states I never imagined could be reached.

The early-morning hours turned very unpleasant; as soon I opened my eyes, a great and impossible to dissipate sorrow appeared. Slowness, fatigue, and apathy remained with me all the time, and accomplishing my responsibilities took superhuman effort. Usually I looked like a *sluggish* person, but the truth was my strength had to be double whenever somebody requested a favor or when something unplanned had to be done. I felt so guilty.

Now the bad humor was part of my daily routine, and, involuntarily, I focused on sadness instead of joy. Tears appeared without calling them. If somebody criticized or turned me down, I would fall into self-rejection, and the only way to find a little relief was sleeping; reaching the limit to stay in bed for entire days with a deep sense of frustration and grief.

Even my personal tastes began to change. The only clothes that called my attention were dark tones or black, and I felt incapable of wearing any bright color. When painting, I could only capture melancholic expressions or desolate gray landscapes. And it became more difficult for me to handle daylight, preferring to stay in darkness and silence.

It that wasn't enough, the constant physical discomfort took me to visit doctors frequently. There were no holes left in my body in which tubes were introduced to find the cause of my afflictions; nevertheless, the diagnosis commonly given in these cases was: "It is just stress, don't you worry."

I started to battle with two personalities: the one that pretended to be normal and the other that trapped me... the one that wished to continue and the other that wanted to sink... the one that understood and the other that was confused... the pleasant one and the unpleasant one. Sometimes, I blamed everything on my zodiac sign "*Gemini*" and the two-figured symbol it represents, but in the end, nothing had logic. And less comprehensible was why that authentic, powerful, and wise *internal voice* could not manage to alleviate my condition.

Having the sensation of carrying a giant stone on my back, I was exhausted from constantly forcing myself to keep going on and pretending to be fine. I began to take the profile of a shy, serious, and unsociable young woman; beginning to think that I was really *crazy* and that there was no cure for my *madness*.

Many times, I wanted to close my eyes and never open them again. The true sense of life was disappearing.

Today I recall a very particular day -after having one of those moments when emotions and reason clash- that I knew the limit had been reached. My body was unresponsive; my mind drove me crazy. I couldn't stand it anymore, and immersed in anguish and weeping, I made the cold determination… to take my own life.

Although it terrified me, I was secure and ready to accomplish my intention. I knew this action, considered by many people to be cowardice, would cause too much damage to my family; however, I thought that showing the real Patricia could be more devastating.

Luckily, the universe played its cards, and at the moment I was ready to take the most crucial step of my existence, the *voice* appeared again. But this time, it didn't speak. This time, it shouted:

- *"NO, NO! Stop! Please don't give up and listen!"*

Refusing to pay attention, I said:

- "I am so sorry, but I have to do it. I can't take it anymore. I am not able to continue. I am tired. Leave me alone!"

I lodged feelings that exceed all limits of understanding. My mind was conscious, but at the same time, it was completely out of reality. A force greater than my capacities pushed me to stop going… to stop being, and the overwhelming mental vibrations encouraging me to keep going… to keep being. There was so much tension between these two energies that I finally lost all vitality, collapsing against the floor and ending immobile and defeated.

The communication continued for a while, until I was calm. Today, I still remember parts of the conversation:

- *"Have you had enough?"* – The voice asked.

- "Have I had enough? Of course I have had enough of everything, and that is why I am doing what I am doing." – I responded.

- *"In fact, what I am trying to ask is if you have had enough of looking for happiness outside yourself? Have you realized that the more you search for security in others… the more it goes away? The more you become obsessed with finding the truth in others… the more it vanishes? The more you undervalue yourself… the more others undervalue you? And when the sense of your own being is lost… the real sense of existence is also lost?*

Are you ready to turn around your life for good? It is your true will to change?"

- "Yes! But, I do not know how." – I affirmed.

- *"The first and most important aspect is the desire that your heart must have for changing, because nothing will be different if you don't decide that it should be.*
Second, take a sheet of paper and a pencil, and write WHO YOU WANT TO BE."

- "I never have known who I am or who I would like to be." – I responded.

- *"Just close your eyes and dream. It is not what others want you to be or what the circumstances have made you to be; it is how 'you' would like to be. Just imagine and write it. The strength and the wisdom are within you. Trust your instincts and never deny the expression of your emotions."*
"If the raw material with which the universe has been created is love, balance, wisdom, abundance, joy, and perfection, and you are one part of the universe not more important that a sand grain but not less valuable than your own creator; then, how can you doubt that 'you' are also love, balance, wisdom, abundance, joy, and perfection?"
"When you recognize your foundation, and your body, mind, and spirit are placed in vibration with the primary essence... when you decide to be what you should be; only then will you begin to feel your reality. The truth is around you, but you listen and understand it inside you."

- "If so, why do I feel so bad?" – I asked.

- *"Your own thoughts are pushing you far away from the original course. You are refusing to accept who you are, denying your true nature and blocking its flow."*

- "What do you mean by 'original course'?" – I interrogated.

- *"Imagine something. At the moment of your birth, you are sitting on a small anchored boat at the source of a great river of water that opens in front of you. Your eyes contemplate a canal shaping the entire torrent flowing ahead, and its image becomes part of the horizon after a long haul. The energy –in this case, the water– runs continuous and smoothly, with the necessary force to drag the boat in the same direction."*

"In the stage of growth when your conscience is expanding and your first moral decision is made, the anchor loosens and your boat begins to follow the current's route. While navigating freely, you may observe, along the banks of the stream, thousands of small 'sites' –one next to the other– which get lost in the distance. Every location offers something different. You can contemplate and recreate yourself with an immense variety of beings, objects, scents, flavors, textures, sounds, thoughts, emotions, sensations, and much more."

"It is like a marketplace that you manage to explore in your watercraft."

"If you wish to take the paddles, move towards the shore, and get down in any of the dwellings that catch your attention, be completely certain that you will find something valuable. Each place visited will provide new supplies that may be kept in your ship and will assure you a good trip... supplies that are essential for continuing down current until reaching the finish line of your river: The Universal Core."

"But, also, it is your decision not to get back in the boat, and instead continue walking deep into a jungle that extends behind the sites. You will be, then, submerged in a strange land full of interwoven obstacles that prevent you from seeing the horizon; and although you try to bring them down, again and again they will reappear. It is an environment in which the conditions are not appropriate, and will make you feel lost, weak, sad, and hopeless, because all the items you need to survive were left in your comfortable mode of transportation!"

"And if after going deeper into the wild, you encounter another river that flows parallel to yours, do not board any other boat you see, since you will be following the pathway that has been designated for another person."

"Each individual has a unique space and their own course to get to the same destiny. And even if, in a certain way, you surrender to the current, it is your personal choice where you want to stop; what you want to feel, learn, or experience; and how long you are going to stay in each location before continuing the journey."

"You are the sole owner of your river and your boat; the performer of your adventure. Furthermore, it is your choice whether or not to navigate this river and face this adventure."

"If you don't decide who you want to be, nobody will do it for you... not even the universe."

During that moment, a feeling of hope appeared like never before. Finally, I confirmed the generator of my transformation was nearer from where I imagined: 'It' was within me. And even if it was still so difficult to understand what exactly *it* was, I have no doubt that it had just saved my life.

I promised myself to never walk again with my head down. I would look straight into people's eyes without fear of being judged for who I was or what I thought. That as much as I respected others, I would respect myself... that the value I gave to others, I would also give to myself... that I would put all my concepts in order and choose those with which I identified... that I would learn to follow my heart for recognizing my true desires, and from then on, even if the trip was difficult, courage would be my unconditional ally to find my destiny.

When writing *"who I wanted to be,"* I began to discover my own reality and experienced much tranquility. But the story of my life didn't end here. Many other events had to happen to generate the wonders of the years to come...

Reflections of My Experience...

During these years, I understood very important concepts.

We, humans, have exactly the same value as each of the elements that form the universe. But there is something that makes us very special. Something that offers us independence to decide who we want to be, what we wish to experience, and how to obtain it: FREE WILL.

It is our will to change or to be stuck in a stormy life. It is an individual decision to be sincere with ourselves or to sink in negative feelings that destroy the true reason for existence. It is a particular choice to fight for turning our dreams into reality or to be fearful when confronting any kind of failure. And, is an exclusive freedom to listen to the wise internal voice that shows us the correct way to achieve plenitude, or to continue with learned behaviors that prevent us from clearly receiving the messages that she transmits.

When we connect with our essence, life is visualized in a more appropriate way. We understand that nobody gives us value; we are born with it. No one grants us the desire to be alive; it is part of ourselves already. Nobody can validate our thoughts; they are supreme and sacred. And don't forget that the force that makes our ideals a reality comes attached to our soul.

Also, I learned that happiness depends on personal determination and is not in the hands of others.

If we allow the truth and positive emotions to be lodged in our interior and healthily get our own respect, having somebody tell us "I love you" won't be necessary. We will not need stimulation to admire a flower, to be fascinated by a full-moon night, to vibrate with music that seduces us to move our body, or perhaps to sing loudly a tune that touches our heart, even if we sound like a record played by an old phonograph.

And if we establish that our joy is not the responsibility of others, we must also accept that neither are our *misfortunes*. Then, when difficult situations or negative people cross our path, we are the only ones responsible for letting our spirit be knocked down; for hiding under the wings of somebody else's thoughts and behaviors; and for searching for who or what should be blamed for our own inability to take control of survival.

A sincere desire is the base of any change, one of the most powerful tools that we have. To decide how to shape our personality and how to face life through the years is a privilege granted to us from birth; but the option to use this non-transferable *free-pass* is totally personal.

The true destiny of humanity is to enjoy a pleasant life. It is the reason we were created and for what we were born. However, even if it is sometimes difficult to accept, we are those who decide to cover our eyes... to close our ears... to seal our mouth... to chain our skin... and to repress our heart.

"During this period of my life, I confirmed that the greatest force of us humans is a powerful and wise energy that lives in the deepest place of our soul. But we have to make the individual choice to keep connected with it or to remain completely disconnected from it."

V
Returning to Be Born

Big changes occurred when I was approximately 17, which filled me with a lively sensation. And realizing the great power I had acquired, the connection with the *internal voice* became stronger.

My first impulse was to read positive-thinking and self-help books. Hundreds of excellent authors offer valuable information in how to build self-esteem; and I am so thankful, with all my heart, to those who encouraged me with their writing at this point of my journey.

Day by day, I gained the courage to express many things that had been kept inside me. I decided to speak, ask, and even discuss any subject. The peculiarity about the situation was that instead of being a shy, quiet, and insecure girl, I became someone who argued with great enthusiasm to prove my points of view. And if there is any doubt, my former high school classmates can give testimony of it, as they surely remember me for all these attributes.

I felt like returning to be born. Now, I didn't worry of telling society regarding my new thoughts and how I would no longer accept many of its conditions.

I also remember unbelievable happiness when the obsession of finding me a rescuer ended. I had understood completely that the famous so long waited Prince Charming didn't live in a distant kingdom, but he had his *private chamber* deep within my soul. Now when boys approached me, I showed an amazing sense of personal security and radiated a different energy that caught the attention of these young Casanovas.

Even if I confess the fear I felt when having the chance for my "first kiss", from which I survived just fine.

But there was one last test that would confirm my newfound internal strength: the day a serious relationship had to be faced and my heart would be totally compromised. I was so worried my old habits would force me to blindly get attached to a partner. Happily, one more time, I attained victory; and when this first relationship ended, I had the strong resolution to continue my stimulating journey.

From then on there were many changes for me: new personality, new country of residence with different language and a better social system; new studies, jobs, loves, and friendships. The metamorphosis was so visible that even the old Ugly Duckling seemed to have transformed into something more attractive. I thank the universe for all those opportunities when I managed to enjoy life as never before.

At last, all appeared back to normal. Like playing again in the magical world of my childhood, I was laughing, singing, dancing, and looking for incentives to hold happiness. I learned to trust my emotions, and intuition started to play a big role in accomplishing my ambitions.

Well! Usually life is simple, but quickly it may turn complicated. When we think we know everything, we find out that we don't know much.

I thought discovering the magical key of my inner self would be more than enough to calm my soul; although, soon I realized that occasionally the shadows from earlier years continued appearing as ghosts. Small details, such as comments, discussions, songs, films, or old memories, abruptly pushed me to deal with past conditions. After feeling a high level of joy, in a matter of seconds, I would fall into sadness and distress.

Oppression in my head and stomach made tears roll down my face, and the sensation of being a stranger reappeared.

I couldn't believe it!

It was impossible to give an explanation for what was wrong with me, so I persistently kept hiding this uncontrollable side of my existence. I got used to live no longer sunk in constant sorrow, but yet dealing with changeable extreme emotional states. One minute I was living; the next one, I was dying.

So far, several acquired elements allowed me to feel better; however, I began to understand that many others were lacking. And with the exceptional aid of my inner force, which encouraged me to follow the course of my destiny, I was ready to persevere in the endless search for this *"something"* that could offer me the stability for always yearned...

Reflections of My Experience...

During these years, I recognized the meaning of an often-heard expression: "*LOVE* is the most powerful force of the universe;" which, sadly, has become a *cliché* and lost its real value.

There is not enough vocabulary to describe the concept of *love*; although, almost everybody can give testimony of the vigor and pleasure generated by it.

One of the most special youthful states occurs when, for first time, the mind becomes conscious of what the heart experiences. Suddenly, at the moment we are sharing with someone else, our being is transported to a world that offers calm and balance. It seems like our senses begin to fly and perceive sensations beyond the surroundings.

Our eyes see things we haven't seen before, our ears catch harmonies that have not been heard, our skin discovers impressions we never imagined, and the heart lodges a joy difficult to exceed. We enter into a magical atmosphere. Comfortable aspects flow naturally, such as tenderness, freedom, humor, cordiality, enthusiasm, and many other that turn any sentimental relationship to *perfect*.

"Well! We are in love."

And, of course, *love* is perfect. However, we humans have distorted not only its meaning but the way it is experienced.

We forget love is the energy or raw material with which the universe was created and it is inherent to humankind. From the moment of birth, we are, we experience, and we radiate this high emotion; and it can be confirmed by watching an image of any newborn child.

Love is born with us and lives in us; it never departs and never arrives.

Unfortunately, many unsuitable habits, ideas, and other factors are acquired as we grow, denying us the enjoyment of perceiving our true essence. And when somebody makes us feel the delicious taste of love again –or maybe as the legend tells, we are crossed by Cupid's arrow and get enchanted by its magical tonic– we become confused and think this "sweetheart" is the real source of our pleasure.

This is why the day our *loved one* is gone, the charming current and the cozy state we had entered disappear. We experience a huge emptiness that brings opposite feelings; sadness, anxiety, humiliation, anger, and even hatred may become part of the difficult situation. So we feel the impulse to bring back and retain the partner at any cost, thinking that her/his company will bring the lost sensation of pleasure *one more time*.

"Love becomes possession."

Perhaps we don't see in our own personality the same capacities and qualities we admire in our *soul mate,* nor did we feel capable of acquiring them. So we get blindly attached to the other person, looking for security and protection, being frightened of losing her/his support.

"Love turns into dependency."

Or maybe when we don't even consider having love for ourselves, we easily become a puppet of anybody who expresses us affection, disregarding disrespect and mistreatment. The self-esteem we had once is now in the hands of that other.

"Love is transformed into shadow."

We must understand that love cannot be captured; it only can be shared. "We really fall in love when I allow the love flowing through me join the love flowing through you. So, there is no possession... no dependency... no shadow... there is no fear of losing this beautiful emotion that circulates within us and never can be taken away from our hearts."

Nobody should have the weight or responsibility of making us happy with their love, much less to be blamed if their hearts no longer vibrate alongside ours. In addition, if our *loved one* has left this physical life, let's just keep the good memories and don't feel drawn by the absence of what still vibrates in our soul.

Love stream flows throughout everything that exists and fulfills us constantly. For this reason, should be very easy to fall in love with our own person; to get enamored with someone special who wants to share with us respectfully and honestly, even if for a short time; to be enchanted by children, family, friends; to be seduced by the sun, water and wind.

"At this point of my trip I learned that when we get conscious of *real love* and integrate it in all aspects of our existence, we can perceive the authentic creator's energy wrapping our being. It is when, truly, we return to being born."

VI
Depression?

The constant search for finding the cause of my afflictions continued with big changes and emotional falls. But, thank God, my inner support continued offering me some clarity to make important life decisions; like the day I wholeheartedly knew, the boy with whom I just had a pleasant conversation, would be in a not too distant future my spouse and the father of my children.

I felt scared, cannot deny it. Nevertheless, I believed with confidence it was the correct choice and the appropriate moment to consolidate a relationship. And this is how, at my twenty-four years of age, back in my homeland, and after one beautiful and joyful reception, I became "*Mrs. Patricia.*"

I found somebody who was self-secure, active, happy, and mainly with a contagious desire for living. Filled with youth and loaded with dreams, we undertook the difficult task of balancing two independent, different, and completely obstinate worlds.

One tiny hope remained deep in my soul that I would finally be fine. But even if I was trying to enjoy all the good things that can be generated from being with a loved one, it was definitely very difficult to hide my uncomfortable situation. I didn't have a room of my own that could offer me shelter as I had in the past; I was no longer completely independent as during my college years; the internal voice was not my companion and confidant anymore, and instead, my new partner began to be my support.

The external pressures started to intensify!

How could I keep covering up or justifying actions that seemed absurd in front of anyone's eyes, including mine? Such as locking myself in a closet, crying because I didn't want to host some friends that we invited for dinner; feeling paralyzed when listening to all of the plans to go to some social event; staying in bed the whole day with a hideous body heaviness and an immense sensation of guilt; or perhaps when, frequently, without justification, an irrational desire came upon me to strike my head against the wall.

How incomprehensible it must be listening to someone who thinks nothing in life makes sense; who is completely insecure and doesn't know where to go; who neither laughs nor dreams; who is incapable of describing her emotions; and worst, who, despite loving and being thankful for everything she has, feels too tired to continue living.

Making an effort to defend some good things that I thought were still part of me, and looking for excuses to justify my *unexplainable* performance, instigated constant marital disputes and created an environment that was far from harmonious. This entire situation recalled my adolescence years and added one heavier than ever load: feeling for the first time my behavior not only was destroying me, but also deeply affecting my husband. And this I couldn't stand!

Again, I sank into a hateful state and lost the little force that had taken. The anxiety pushed me to try one more time the frightful step I attempted in the past, from which I had miraculously been saved.

Even if my connection with the *voice* had greatly decreased, I held strong, and took a not so devastating but still drastic determination that seemed to be the last solution on my list: to visit a psychiatrist and be locked up at a mental institution, wrapped in a straitjacket.

"What else can be done? Definitely I am crazy and there is no cure for me." – I thought.

So my story continued!

I randomly chose a physician who I considered at that moment of my life to be a "crazy people specialist," and requested an appointment. Today I recall the strange sensation I had when entering the dark office of that eccentric looking man, who was waiting for me on the other side of his shabby desk.

When hearing the typical question: "Tell me what is happening to you?" I gave a great sigh and fell into a discouraged silence. How can I answer the question that has been with me during many years and for which there is no explanation? How can I explain *what is happening to me?* Where should I begin? How can I bring to light all of the stormy things I never had the courage to show even to closest people? How long would take me to tell the complete story? – I meditated for a few minutes.

Thinking this was my last chance, I began to speak. But maybe just five minutes had passed of me describing my complicated situation, when the doctor interrupted:

- *"Do not worry. I know what your problem is, and it is very easy to fix."*

I was astonished and believed my ears were failing.

- "What?" – I questioned with a surprised tone.

- *"DEPRESSION is what you have."* – The doctor said.

- "DEPRESSION?" – I asked.

- *"Yes. DEPRESSION! Have you ever heard this term before?"*

- "No." – I answered.

- *"You suffer from a condition called Depression. It manifests in several ways and yours could be classified as Maniac-Depressive. I am going to send you some medicine and, in around a week, everything will be fine."* – The doctor affirmed, as he opened the desk drawer and took out a small box with caplets."

I felt such a hard impact from his words that get hit on my head with a baseball bat would have been easier to handle. I couldn't understand what I was listening, and as something unusual, a hearty laugh involuntary came.

- *"What happened?"* – He asked with surprise.

- "Are you saying something I have been struggling with for so long and putting all my determination to defeat will disappear in one week just by taking some pills?" – I questioned in a mocking way.

- *"Madam, please allow me to be sincere. When you came through that door, I never thought you would say what you just said. The situation you experienced generally drags people to fall into states of alcoholism, drug addiction, other disorders, or even confinement in psychiatric hospitals. I don't understand how you avoided these conditions and manage to look like a normal person."*

- "Doctor, with all respect," – I asked a little more seriously. "We are not talking about a *toothache* that may be calmed with an analgesic. Do you want me to believe some 'pills' will transform my way of being, thinking, and feeling?"

- *"I see."* – The psychiatrist affirmed with a slight smile – *"You will not use the medication, doubting its effectiveness, right? So let's make a deal. Promise me that for at least seven straight days, you will take the pills and wait to see what happens. Please do it for me, if you don't want to do it for yourself."*

"One specific dose of the medicine has to be given to each patient. If there is not improvement or you feel worse, we may have to combine it with another prescription, until we get the right dosage. Okay?
Do not worry; everything is going to be fine."

- "Okay. If I accept, for how long would I have to take it?" – I asked.

- *"Indefinitely."* – He answered.

I didn't know what to think or say. For the first time somebody was giving me a solution to my problem; however, it was difficult to absorb that I had a *disease* like many other people, and, perhaps, the only solution was to consume medication for the rest of my life.

Without a better option and barely excited, I decided to accept the deal.

I bought the supposed *"magical pills,"* which would fix the circumstances. In the beginning, my being fell into terrible states, even worse than before; but as promised, I called the doctor and he prescribed another medicine to combine with the first one.

With surprise I began feeling better in a matter of days, as he foretold. My body recovered some energy and seemed less heavy. The anxiety and distresses were vanishing, and sadness no longer marked my face in such an abrupt way. In addition, like a blessing from the sky, the headaches disappeared.

At least the term "crazy" had been changed for "depressive," offering me some comfort and hope.

Hope again... hope for finding the solution... hope for finally changing my life forever.

I cannot deny that for a long time the medications covered my condition and somehow stabilized me, but a large amount of negative symptoms remained hidden and anguished thoughts continued bumping.

Sadly, without understanding the true sense of what was happening, my crooked pathway did not finish here either. Although the weight was lightened, I still needed to go through many events and understand many more, to find an effective way that would pull up the problem by its roots...

Reflections of My Experience...

During this period, I turned my interest in everything referring to Depression and started to learn about the subject.

I found that not long ago Depression was classified as a disorder or illness that causes emotional, mental, and physical instability. According to medicine, it could be caused by an imbalance in some chemical substances of the brain; it could be acquired by genetic inheritance, and even if managed, it could be very difficult to cure.

Under terms like bipolar, maniac-depressive, chronic depression, and others, the treatment of Depression was generally reduced to medications consumption. Eventually, a great variety of products began to appear in the market: prescribed ones and others labeled as *natural* that supposedly induce happiness. Also, in severe cases, extreme methods were used, such as electroconvulsive therapy that induces "electric shocks" to the patient's brain.

Psychology field also offered some therapies, but they were usually long term and accompanied with medications.

Even with all this information, there was not much clarity about the description, true cause, or an effective treatment to end this *strange* condition. So, based on all the years of experiencing it, I decided to shape my own concept of Depression in the following words:

Depression seems to be a set of negative manifestations that appear in the different aspects of a person's life; and, step by step, not only the personal development is affected, but also their performance with the rest of the world.

Some of the symptoms are:

- Sadness and bitterness
- Constant desire to cry
- Anguish
- Fear
- Susceptibility
- Irritability
- Abrupt mood changes
- Heart Oppression
- Constant desire to sleep or insomnia
- Little appetite or extreme urge to eat
- Loss of memory and concentration
- Exhaustion and lack of interest in any type of physical activity
- Lack of sexual appetite or extreme sexuality
- General discomfort without specific cause
- Frequent headaches or migraines
- Hopelessness and self-rejection
- Tendency to magnify difficulties
- Solitary
- Pessimistic thoughts and feelings of culpability
- Desire to die and, many times, suicidal actions

A case of Depression may express only a few of the above symptoms, or conversely most, if not all of them. The intensity may differ on a scale from slight to medium to very intense. So, a symptom may quickly go from one level to other, or may change abruptly from one emotion into an opposite one.

"In a matter of seconds a little blue becomes a deep sadness... or a great joy in weeping."

I would divide Depression into two groups: the Justified and the Unjustified.

Justified Depression: The name says everything. This Depression has some *justification* because the person faces traumatic events such as death of a loved one, physical mistreatment, serious disease, disability, bankruptcy, broken heart, or entering stages of great changes such as adolescence and elderly.

Identifying the origin or cause of *Justified Depression* is simple. And frequently the individual recovers the natural life disposition little by little, with professional aid or simply thanks to the reassuring touch of time.

Unjustified Depression: This one is very common and affects modern society mostly. Every day, in each corner of our planet, millions of people –without regard for race, gender, or age– fall into depressive states for no apparent reason.

Slowly and smoothly the negative symptoms begin to interlace with people's personality, affecting their emotional and physical balance; and although sometimes some factors may be blamed for this condition, it almost always appears unjustifiable.

Unjustified Depression is very difficult to identify and is often treated only when it reaches extreme levels. Unfortunately, meanwhile most people face *low* levels of Depression, preventing them from recognizing that there is a problem; even if, silently, it damages their physical condition, their perception of the world, and their social performance in an almost permanent way. This is why it is so common to hear phrases such as "I am cranky and I never will change," "I always have bad luck," "I cannot find the course for my life," "Sadness and failure is who I am," and "Nothing makes sense."

However, we must pay close attention to the fact that *depressive states* have always been part of humanity. Throughout history, a large number of personalities have taken their own lives in moments of hopelessness and confusion; many philosophers from ancient times offered their best words to describe "melancholy"; others, named *existentialists,* lived turbulent existences; and some are remembered as having died from *sadness,* submerged in great sorrows because of love.

All this can lead us to think that seeing people full of problems, with conflicts and afflictions, a poor life attitude, and almost zero capacity to enjoy what they do is something natural. We may even think the true role of mankind is suffering, distresses, and pain… that it is our essence… that there is very little to do… that the only way out is to simply continue holding on to this long existence and hoping its end will arrive soon.

Fortunately, for me, nothing of this was logical. It didn't make much sense to call a condition that displays such wide, variable, and contradictory range of symptoms a "disease". It was not easy to accept that throughout history a high percentage of people have suffered from the same "disorder." Or how to explain why so many inhabitants from countries that face strong and prolonged winters are affected by depressive states, but, peculiarly, get better as the climate gets warmer? Or why a happy mom can fall into extreme sadness after childbirth? Or how such special beings as *children* can be diagnosed with Depression, because they have been losing passion for life?

My heart kept telling me something was missing… something we were not understanding… something beyond conventional explanations that, perhaps, we had left back in human evolution… something we had to continue looking for, and maybe someday, manage to recover.

"During these years of my journey, I understood *depressive states* are common occurrences of our species; nevertheless, we do not understand them completely nor do we treat them effectively, so they continue running our lives and shadowing our destinies."

VII
Contradictory Motherhood

In this stage, learning many aspects about Depression lightened part of the weight I was carrying. In addition, like never before, I began to listen with more frequency about other people who were also facing this disturbance.

It seems like being *depressed* was *in fashion.*

Although a kind of shadow remained over me, the medications I was taking managed to stabilize and relax me a little, allowing me to live life in the best possible way between work and marriage.

The connection with the internal voice remained debilitated, but I remember a very special moment when in my mind appeared a powerful affirmation: *"You are ready... ready to be a mom."*

It couldn't be possible. If something I was afraid of was precisely being a mother, and during times of extreme sorrow I considered never becoming one. How could I take responsibility for another person when I was not even able to face my own life? How could innocent beings be brought into this painful and distress world? How could the universe be telling me I was ready to be a mom?

As always, fear and confusion came back to me.

Immediately mental images appeared of big-belly ladies, walking as "Mrs. Ducks," and having extreme midnight cravings that drive husbands crazy; and the unmistakable silly faces of new parents overloaded with backpacks, bottles, diapers, strollers, and the inevitable *arsenal* to stay afloat in the complicated task of having a baby.

- "No! I am not ready." - I stated.

However a pleasant, magical, and difficult to describe energy surrounded me; acquiring inner peace and a strong conviction that indeed I was ready, and very soon I would be giving birth. Thus I embraced this new adventure in my 27 years of age. After nine months of big-belly, walking like "Mrs. Duck," luckily just few cravings, and a labor with several ups and downs, I became a *mom*.

To be honest, I never imagined feeling this incredible emotion of having my little girl in my arms and witnessed the happiness she brought to our family. And even less I dreamed I would experience the same beautiful sensation five years later, when giving birth to my baby boy.

Only a woman who has gone through pregnancy can understand the unbelievable emotion produced by this being growing and anxiously moving within her; awakening the maternal instinct, even if it is completely asleep; making any sensation other than love, tenderness, and amazement to fade away.

We experience a fear that is not fear... a pain that is not pain... a special and powerful force, which, definitively, confirms that *yes* there is something beyond us in the universe generating the current where our boat floats.

Today I still thank God for giving me the privilege to live the miracle of conception.

Well! But life is like a *roller-coaster*; after being on the upper part of the track, it falls with so much power that may terrify and often immobilize us. Because of my pregnancy and other reasons I don't remember clearly I had to suspend the anti-depressive medications, so following the joyful new-mom stage, the negative symptoms returned more overwhelming than before.

During pregnancy, the female body not only undergoes an external transformation, but internally many of the vital organs must move to create a space for the growing baby. The child needs to absorb all food and all energy the mother has available, even if sometimes it jeopardizes her own stability.

A tiny being that develops in her womb; feeds and breathes thanks to her; gets protected by her; and in addition, at birth takes away part of her. This is why it is common for women to experience a strong physical and emotional imbalance after delivery: nervousness, susceptibility, constant desire to cry, tension, and let's not forget the confusion that the newborn requirements produce on the whole family atmosphere.

I remembered the anguish my husband and I felt about not knowing how to take good care of our children. We tried to read their minds to figure out why they were crying, and if our parental instincts failed, we fed them when they were cold and covered them with a warm blanket when they were hungry.

Thus after two pregnancies, the fear, irritability, and impatience returned to mark my behavior. Incapable of understanding the world of my children, I had a lack of energy to follow their activities. It was a paradox; a contradiction. Simultaneously with the happiness of having my children, I felt overwhelmed by the arduous task of being a mom all day long. I thought after finally beginning to enjoy many aspects of life, I was now reduced to remain within four walls, playing childish games, and forced to use an unknown kids' psychology.

Over the years my children were growing, it was very difficult for me to create a calm home environment. Most of the time I was trying to accommodate them into my world... incapable of fitting into their world.

I didn't want to feel overloaded with responsibility, but I did it. I didn't wish to be in bad mood constantly, but I looked for excuses to justify my frustration. I didn't want to think in the incapacity to achieve my personal goals, but, repeatedly, I was questioning myself about it. And much less I didn't desire to continue feeling this *existential distress*, but it remained tearing off my heart.

The new medications were not enough to alleviate the anxiety. The relationship with my husband was deteriorating. My children's behavior began to transform into defensive, disobedient, and aggressive. In general, the atmosphere in our home was perceived as heavy and tense.

Seeing how this stormy state was involving –as I expected– not only to my partner but also to my two *little treasures,* hurt me. I had to force myself to be a good mother and wife; to be a good daughter and sister; to keep myself alive. And only because of the love and respect toward all my dearest people, I did continue the arduous fight to overcome this situation. A slight feeling remained in the deepest place of my soul that urged me to continue looking for a solution, yet with disappointment.

But what I didn't anticipate was that the universe would return on my rescue, and, very soon, great positive changes would begin. Those changes yearned for so long…

Reflections of My Experience...

During these years, in spite of my exhausting situation, I realized that each stage of our journey brings an enormous and particular teaching.

If something appears to be by its own value the most complete and enriching experience, for us humans, it is *parenthood*. And when talking about being a mother or a father, we not only must think in people who are physically capable of conceiving a baby, but also consider those who somehow are in charge of children and share with them the great adventure of their development.

Raising children tests us in aspects like sacrifice, discipline, dedication, and responsibility; raising children also gives us the wonderful opportunity to contact the creatures that radiate the *true essence* of our species and make us recognize how far we, as adults, have moved away from it.

Daily interaction with the little ones shows us all the important tools left behind throughout our growth. They are the only ones who stand in contrast to our acquired attitudes that are pushing us down to live in a world so different from we should; they, and only they, can demonstrate how incapable we have become of laughing, dreaming, loving, expressing, sharing... how incapable we have become of searching for happiness with curiosity and persistence.

Often, some parents hiding behind their work or individual activities try to avoid raising their kids. But whoever foolishly wants to skip the task of supporting and educating children, sooner or later life will make them face their own kids or someone else's, since the parenthood experience is a universal requirement in our evolutionary process. And this should not sound like a threat for those who run away from their responsibilities, but to make them realize that, although being a parent is one of the most complex experiences of our existence, we must face it with integrity and gratefulness.

Also, there is hope for individuals who in this physical or material state don't have the opportunity to be parents/guardians even if they wanted to, because for sure in another phase of existence, the universe will offer them a *second chance* to live and to take advantage of it.

"During these years I comprehended that when we grow apart from the original essence, more conflict and distance toward kids is created. And the more we want to force them to change their authentic and peculiar nature, the more we drag them, along with us, to enter the tangled jungle of this confused society."

VIII
The Beginning
of Change

Generally, when we deal with aspects that impact us strongly, significant changes take place in our thoughts and emotions. As my personal battle continued –after I turned 30 years old– and desperate to find solutions, I experienced an unusual event, relevant for beginning my great change.

A young *clairvoyant-fortune-teller* convinced me that the voice I had been listening and my confusion were originated by a *harmful and obsessed spirit*, which was influencing me to take my own life. And although, deep in my soul, I knew this was not true; amid the desperation, I agreed to be part of a "cleansing ritual" that supposedly would alleviate my restless situation.

This is how I ended up surrounded by several people in a small room, with many crosses, candles, images of saints, and other pieces related to "Santeria." Later, after some introductory words, strange events began to occur when the gentleman who was in charge of *the ritual* apparently was possessed by the spirit. His voice and behavior were transformed, intimidating me with insults and threatening attitudes. Imperceptible forces made some of the objects fly through the air and violently struck the young man several times against the walls.

Between shouts and weeping, other frightful episodes occurred beyond understanding, creating a feeling of panic and disorientation. At the end, the beaten man was left on the floor almost unconscious, and the tense atmosphere vanished when his conduct returned to normal. Supposedly, the undesired spirit had lost the battle and would go away forever, leaving me free of afflictions.

That night we returned to the clairvoyant's house, and one of her friends *channeled* the energy of two different spiritual beings that transmitted beautiful messages about my situation, offering a much more calm experience than I had had earlier.

Everything just happened was so confused and strange that left me with great doubt about whether it was real or part of a horror movie. I tried to find an explanation from a variety of religious representatives and some other recognized people; however, their opinions and recommendations were so contradictory and absurd that pushed my condition to the edge… to the edge of an emotional breakdown in a hospital emergency room, where shouting and kicking I tried to prevent the nurses from injecting me tranquilizers.

On top of this, for the first time, my lamentable state was exposed. The mask had fallen; the secret had been revealed. Thinking everybody around would perceive me as an unbalanced person without cure, produced so much more pain. Thankfully, the unconditional support of my beautiful family helped me to retake the forces for continuing my heterogeneous pathway.

During the entire intensive search for solutions to my depressive episodes, this ritual was the most *radical and insane* action I had ever tried, and certainly was not the answer to the problem either. Nevertheless, I have to acknowledge that it gave me some ingredients to perceive in a different way the connection we have with other types of universal energies, and to be open minded for welcoming the gift that was about to arrive in my hands.

And I don't have a better word than *gift* to refer to the *book* I received by particular circumstances, after resting for more than one week in my parent's house, begging God for help: "The Urantia Book."

"The Urantia Book" is a publication with almost 200 documents across 2,000 pages, considered to be one of the greatest last-given "revelations" to humanity. Transcribed during mid-twentieth century, this masterpiece describes the origin, composition, distribution, and purpose of the entire universe.

After reading it, I understood our planet's controversial history. I understood the reasons why we erroneously think we are alone in this immense universe, the countless entities that compose the complex celestial order, the energy circuits that connect us with the cosmos, the different states of consciousness we may acquire in our existential progress, the important role of human beings in this evolutionary race, and hundreds of more fascinating subjects that satisfied my appetite for knowledge.

Finally, all of my questions had completely logical and convincing answers. Most of my concepts were reinforced and presented as truth, and many other new ones I had never considered, became part of my intellectual repertoire.

But among all this amazing information, something deeply touched my heart: the description of the non-personal (pre-personal) highest spiritual tool humans may receive directly from God, "*The Thought Adjuster.*" This *divine device or monitor* starts to work in each person's mind when the first moral decision is made during the early years of childhood. Loaded with exclusive information, *The Thought Adjuster* has the capacity to be associated with our intellect -if we allow it- and to adjust, uplift, and level off our concepts. It even has the sacred aptitude to wisely guide us for developing and continuing our spiritual evolution in the best way possible.

Most interesting was the explanation of how the *conscious* connection between human reason and the divine monitor engages in a *"dialogue"* that accommodates our ideas logically and progressively. Although, when preconceived and erroneous personal concepts interfere with the complete understanding of new ideas sent by the Adjuster, we may enter into states of great confusion.

Perhaps this was the "*lost link*" I was searching for... perhaps I was not playing with an imaginary friend or the harmful spirit who wanted to drag me down didn't exist... perhaps, this special and unique Adjuster, combined with other components that help mental progress, was the mysterious *voice* residing in my head so long ago.

When this information matched with my own experience, immediately became my truth. I realized the *internal voice* I had tried to extinguish before was an ally instead of an enemy; that I should *re-connect* myself with it and be more prepared to assimilate the conversations.

So finally, I could assure that in fact I was not crazy!

The first thing I did was resume the habit of searching for calm and pleasant places, to make contact not only with my inner self, but with other cosmic energies. Dusting off something had been trapped among the *webs* of forgetfulness for more than five years, wasn't easy, and many days passed in a great silence.

Today, I remember one night being in company of my little daughter while she was falling asleep. When I was about to join her in the world of dreams, something resounded in my mind that shook me up:

- *"Do you remember, several years ago, when I asked you to write on a sheet of paper who you want to be?"* – The voice said.

- "Yes!" – I answered, with great emotion.

- *"Now, I ask you to write: WHAT DO YOU WANT TO ACCOMPLISH IN YOUR LIFE."*

- "I really don't know what I want." – I astonished commented.

- *"If you are not sure what do you want; at least, identify what it is that you don't want."*

"While keeping the vision of your real wishes, with tranquility and security, you will remain in your river. When the true desire is interrupted with fear and doubt of achievement, your life will overflow into the dense jungles. When establishing your goals and yearnings, the universe will immediately take measures for you to retake the course and experience your own existence."

"For so long you have been sailing in someone else's boat, and although it feels comfortable and many things have been learned, you must return to your exclusive destiny. Remember, people paths must go parallel; never interfering with each other's and never using the same trail."

"One of the purpose of existence is to look for your own truth; choosing authentic thoughts, emotions, and behaviors that offer satisfaction. Every truth is sacred, and even if you cannot be mistakenly disrespectful trying to impose your beliefs on others, neither can you darken your own experiences by living the truth of others. Understand that you were created to be delighted with your soul's noble wishes; if they are not accomplished, it is because you insist

on denying what you purely are. Open your mind and heart, and let your original essence flows."

"When you enjoy simple things and choose happiness... when you learn to identify what elevates your spirit or what knocks it down... when you understand that the authentic sense of life is not exactly what we do, but how we do it... and when you expand your conscience and identify your truth, fullness is experienced."

"Your truth will be recognized when you feel no fear, no doubts, no emptiness; otherwise, be sure that you still are very far from it."

I couldn't believe it. I was completely full of emotion and gratitude, seeing how this divine energy had embraced me again. And after thinking a while, I affirmed:

- "Yes! There is something I wish: Learn to be happy. Understand why I am depressed all the time despite having so many pretty things around. Identify the real causes which incapacitate me from living and find ways to overcome them."

- *"First, I want you to understand. You cannot learn to be happy; you can only return to be happy!*

"You were born with happiness within you, and simply have to be recovered. The negative things are illusions; the positive things are your reality. And it is your decision which ones you want to confront."

"Second, all data referring existence is engraved in the cosmic circuits. The universe is the best teacher in your road of learning; the one that stimulates your growth and development. Just get connected with it, and at any moment, you will obtain the answers you have been waiting for so long."

From then on, I saw perfectly how I had been mistaken. I realized the *internal voice* never confused me; I had confused myself. It never left me; I had turned my back on it. And no one else but me had prevented it from trying to improve my life.

I began to meditate daily and started to receive new information, as I was younger. Now, with fortune, I was better capable to freely and naturally participate in the dialogue, obtaining its true benefits.

It seems like an open water tap running a stream of ideas into my head that had to be processed by my intellect. It took several months of work and many night getting ups to write everything was coming in, which had to be logically organized and interpreted in the morning.

To explain how all this information arrived in my head is a little complicated. I just may say the new ideas introduced through the dialogues, were mixed with others I had acquired during previous years; and much more that had been covered by *"spider webs"* in the *"corners"* of my subconscious were also added. At the end, somehow, everything was joined and gave me a very different approach to Depression than before.

All the puzzle pieces, randomly dispersed during my life, were put together to show a new image. And at last, a complete overview could be visualized.

In the following chapters, I will try to transcribe everything assimilated back then. It is not easy to explain such complex concepts that maybe are new for many of you; but I am convinced when our minds are open for analyzing a wide range of ideas, we can better understand the processes of existence and produce regenerative changes.

SECOND PART

ᔕ ᔕ ᔕ ᔕ ᔕ ᔕ

Congratulations! You have reached the awaited point at the journey of reading this book where you will understand not just, how I transformed my life, but also how you will manage to transform yours.

I am sure this perspective about Depression is very different from you have heard until now. This is a *particular, natural, and integral* perspective, and let me say, a much more *refreshing* point of view than the traditional one.

"Particular" because it shows my own experience when dealing and healing Depression. "Natural" because the fact that we are energetic creatures with an individual frequency, which changes according to our life habits and the interaction we have with surrounding natural elements. "Integral" because the three essential energy currents of human beings – physical, mental, spiritual– are exposed, describing the conditions generated to us when each *energy flow* falls in decreasing ranges and lose tuning.

A vision that makes total sense for me and was a decisive and irreplaceable key to climbing out from the hole of Depression… the hole where I would never return!

IX
Understanding Depression

Depression is the set of negative conditions or symptoms acquired when our vital energies lose tuning as they enter into low vibration energetic ranges, away from our optimum or initial frequency.

I guess what you are thinking: "What? Pardon me? What did she say?"

But, don't you worry. I progressively explain, and you will see it is much simpler than it sounds.

Let's begin with the basics...

Our Energy

To expose the energy subject in scientific terms is complicated, so this is why I express myself in an elementary and sometimes metaphoric form.

To understand any aspect referring to *existence*, especially about human beings, it is necessary to consider a very important fact: "Absolutely everything that exists is *energy* manifested in infinite frequencies of vibration."

Energy means *life,* which is described as the movement of the most essential particles in the universe called atoms. All atoms have a distinct oscillating movement named *vibration.* And vibration can occur at different speeds –according to a specific period of time– creating frequency.

So, let's say for producing *life or energy* there must be movement... there must be vibration.

Now, imagine the center of the universe as a great volcano. From its wide crater, a gaseous, dense, and fine matter called "Universal Energy" constantly emanates; resembling a big cloud that slowly expands throughout space, like filling the infinite.

As this Universal Energy starts to move away from the volcano on a long journey, it manifests itself in diverse ways. With a specific initial frequency, the speed, size, and position of its small atoms change gradually; and second by second, something new is created.

This is how every object, being, color, scent, texture, flavor, sound, and the rest of the elements have a *unique* oscillation that allows each one to display particular characteristics; similar to barcodes that identify items for selling or the fingerprints that determine every person's individuality.

Everything, absolutely everything, in the cosmos has the same raw material exposed in different frequencies of vibration; forming an enormous *spectrum* in which high frequencies diminish to low frequencies.

Elements of similar composition form smaller *scales*, equally arranged in progressive frequencies. For example, if we observe the "Light Spectrum," each color has its own place next to other; delicately gliding from light tones to middle and then to dark ones. (See graphic No. 1)

Graphic No. 1

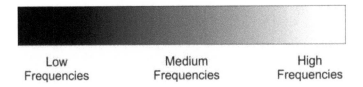

| Low
Frequencies | Medium
Frequencies | High
Frequencies |

Or flavors series begins with sweets, going through salty, and then acidic, according to their point of vibration. Sounds are manifested in high, mid, or low depending on their frequency. Solid elements have lower vibration speed than liquids; and gases maintain even higher vibration than liquids. Hot temperatures indicate greater oscillations; cold temperatures, smaller oscillations. Even living beings have ranges; thus some animals and plants are developed in quick velocity, and others such as fungi, bacteria, and viruses get life at very slow velocity.

And the classification can continue indefinitely.

Well, *people* are not an exception from this arrangement. After all we also belong to the magnificent creation and enjoy an important place in this infinite arena of contrasts.

The human species also has the "Universal Energy" as its essential matter, forming a particular scale or mini-spectrum where each individual occupies an exclusive frequency position.
(See graphic No. 2)

Graphic No. 2

At the moment of our conception, the universe assigns us an *individual* space with a *unique* frequency, allowing our energy to manifest in a completely original way.

Bio-Antenna Effect

The fact we are energy beings vibrating in a particular frequency creates an "effect" that I call "Bio-Antenna." This is because we have the ability to *transmit* energy outwards from our body and also to *receive* energy from the external world. In other words, we are "biological antennas" that handle one *private connection* with the rest of the universe.

Let me use an example for better understanding:

Think about a simple manual radio: a non-digital device, without an automatic finder or *scanner,* which has to be manually operated for locating radio stations. A technology from a not-so-old generation like mine that unfortunately seems almost obsolete in these days of rapidly growing communication. (See graphic No. 3)

Graphic No. 3

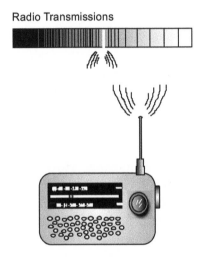

Radio Transmissions

The small radio or *machine* supports all necessary pieces to catch the emissions spread throughout air: A *power button* that allows the machine to be turned on or off. An *antenna* that can produce a range of waves with different frequencies, as well as capture waves generated by the stations. A *tuner knob* or *dial,* which moves from side to side, enables locating the different stations available. An *amplifier* or *loudspeaker* that reproduces currents caught by the antenna. A *volume* system that gives the option of listening to sound at various levels of intensity. And a *battery* or *cord* that generates electric impulse for all the preceding elements to work properly, completing the transistor's purpose of broadcasting transmissions produced at great distance.

Now! As extraordinary beings, we behave in the same way as radios!

Our *physical body* is like the radio-machine. Our *thoughts,* acting like an antenna, create different vibrations and connect with analogous emissions radiated by the Mental Energy that flows across the cosmos. Our *free will* is the tuner knob used to choose universal frequencies with which we want to be in tune. Our *emotions* −as music sounds through loudspeaker− are result of transmissions caught by our thoughts from the universe. How *intensely* or *freely* we express our feelings can be compared to the radio's volume. And the *stimulation* we give to ourselves to remain active, is similar to the battery or electrical flow.

In Tune

Let's say the radio is on. The dial is located at the point numbered "96.3 FM," corresponding to a *classical music* station. The antenna begins to generate radio waves or vibrations at the indicated frequency, immediately connecting to equivalent waves transmitted by the music station. This way when the two radio-electric signals of exact frequency match, an aerial channel for which the sound is transported from the station to the radio is open. Finally, the music is amplified by the speaker in the intensity indicated by the radio's volume control.

If the classical music is clearly heard –without any trace of static or sound from other station– we may say the radio is "in tune." To obtain a true tuning, there are two conditions that need to be met: First, the machine has to receive the correct energetic stimulus from the electric system or a fully loaded battery; and, second, the dial must be perfectly aligned with "96.3 FM" indicator, so the antenna can emit an equivalent frequency to the one transmitted by the radio station.

Exactly like radio-antennas we humans have the ability to connect with three "stations" or universal energy circuits, named: Material, Mental, and Spiritual. (See graphic No. 4)

Graphic No. 4

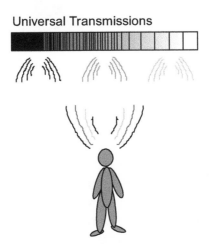

Universal Transmissions

In the moment of our conception, a spark of vibration is produced in our mother's womb, giving initial impulse to ignite the "radio" and open a bridge or connection to the *Material* energy. Soon, as we grow and acquire a higher frequency, we perceive the *Mental* circuit. And, finally, to catch the *Spiritual* station, we must reach a point of much greater vibration.

Here is when we consider that human beings are not uni-dimensional, but tri-dimensional, because we are the interaction of three powerful currents of energy that must work together in complete coordination. (See graphic No. 5)

Graphic No. 5

And even if the three currents work in complete coordination, at the same time each one vibrates at an independent frequency, with unique functions and characteristics. As follows:

- *Material Energy*: it may be visualized as a huge "red color" cloud expanding throughout space. This current manifests our physical body, allowing us to perceive the external world with the senses of smell, taste, hearing, touch, and sight.

- *Mental Energy*: it may be visualized as a great "yellow color" mist where all the memories of the universe are registered. It gives our brain the material to generate thoughts, ideas, and concepts needed for us to understand how to interact and survive the physical world.

- *Spiritual Energy*: it may be visualized as a beautiful "blue color" river of energy, through which we connect with much-higher frequencies than those offered by the Mental current. It offers the most altruistic and noble ideals of our existence, and expands our consciousness to distinguish correct from incorrect, real from unreal, truth from illusion, life from expiration.

In the next chapters these three primary or essential energies will be more deeply presented.

Meanwhile, let's say that as radio-antennas, our machinery (body, mind, and spirit) must produce *equivalent* vibration frequencies to each one of the three main currents, in order for us to get in tune with them.

The good condition of our body is subject to a correct Physical Energy vibrational level, offering us vitality and health. The appropriate performance of our mind depends on the right Mental Energy flowing maintained by the brain, bringing us an agile and creative intellect. And our spirit is fed by the amount of information circulating through the Spiritual Current, flooding us with higher wisdom that directly arrives from The Creator's force.

We are pure energy connected with central universal powers by way of specific frequencies. But we must be in tune with them to catch the necessary information that assures a suitable corporal, mental, and spiritual performance.

Out of Tune

If for any reason there is not enough electricity or battery to power the radio, the transmission we are listening to begins to distort and loses connection. Or if the *dial* is moved, even a millimeter, from the exact frequency, the components of the music start to fade and harmony is replaced by a rainy noise. Here it may be said, the radio is "out of tune."

In the same way, if *our* energy changes the original frequency that produces a correct connection, we enter into an interference field and fail to keep communication with the universal sources. If our being doesn't maintain a specific amount of energy or our battery goes down, we begin to lose all positive aspects and perceive others instead that produce confusion and distortion of reality. Our "inner fire" starts to extinguish.

Consequently, the physical body runs out of vigor and begins to form strange conditions like diseases. Thoughts, ideas, and concepts no longer flow easily, leading us to make incorrect decisions, which affect our good social performance and appropriate interaction with the world around. Likewise the bond with *God* starts to disappear, causing us to misinterpret life's true sense and perceive ourselves anguished, abandoned, and without hope.

If our vibration is suitable, we receive positive stimulation from the universe; but if our vibration is unsuitable, we lose it.

Now, to better understand how we get out of tune from the universal forces, it is necessary to speak about something I call "Frequential Space;" defined as the area, section, or energy field of the universal spectrum where each existing element belongs.

If we use a piano instrument as analogy, we can visualize every one of the *keys* as a Frequential Space in the *keyboard* scale.

Each Frequential Field is formed by three internal parts:

1- *Optimal Point or Midpoint:* located in the middle of the section, it is where the element energy vibrates at 100%. (See graphic No. 6)

2- *Decreasing Space:* field that extends towards one side of the midpoint in which frequency declines. Here, the energy waves generated by the element's core gradually lessen intensity, until vanishing completely in the next Frequential Space of the spectrum.

3- *Increasing Space:* field that expands from the midpoint towards other direction of the scale where vibrations rise. Here, the element's core energy waves gradually increase intensity until arriving at the adjacent Frequential Space of the spectrum.

Graphic No. 6

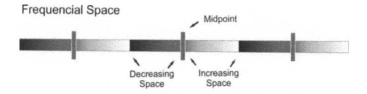

Let's go back to the radio communication example!

In communications wide range, a specific aerial strip for transmitting its own information is assigned to every radio station. Each aerial band acts as a Frequential Space, having a midpoint at which the emission is transmitted in an integral and perfect way, and two adjacent areas where the signal starts to lose all its qualities. Frequential Fields manifest since the moment any broadcast leaves the radio station, until radio devices are reached.

This way, if the radio device is tuned to the correct frequency "96.3 FM" –our favorite classical music station– the sound will be vivid, clear, and exact. But if the dial button is moved towards lower frequencies side, a rain of noise begins to distort the *purity* of the original music. The melody progressively vanishes, the instruments disappear one by one, and volume intensity lowers until the connection completely finishes.

If, delicately, we continued moving the knob in the same direction, the next Frequential Space –from a different station– will be reached; perhaps a sports network that has its own channel at "95.8 FM," beside the classical music radio band, will bring us new sounds.

Now, if we tune in back the music station, but this time move the dial towards the other side, into higher frequencies, the previous phenomenon will take place again. Little by little the classical tune signal will be lost, until the information transmitted by the adjacent frequency "97.5 FM" is reached, which in this case belongs to a *News* station.

So the music station's Frequential Space begins at the point where *sports* are broadcast, continues until *perfect tuning*, and ends in the other side when the *news* zone interposes.

The beautiful symphony loses all its core original components when on one side is replaced by the commentator shout of "Gooo…oaal!" announcing the local soccer team's score; and, on the other side, by the voice of the analyst giving an economic report.

When its vibrations are diminished, or by the contrary over-stimulated, the music gradually becomes noise; until it stops being music… until it disappears.

And once more, we must look at human being wonders!

In our corresponding dimension, and as creatures of energy nature, we also manifest in Frequential Spaces.

We express an *Optimal Point* of frequency when our energy vibrates in an integral condition or 100%; a *Decreasing Space,* in which our vibrations decline until 0%; and an *Increasing Space,* in which our energy raises until the limit to be off its own place… off its own manifestation.   (See graphic No. 7)

Graphic No. 7

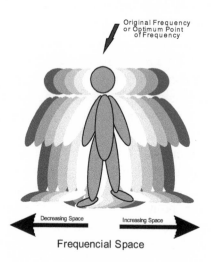

As I already explained, everything works well if our energy vibrates in exact frequency of the universal sources. But if our energy goes out of tune, then our personal conditions will change.

If we don't stimulate ourselves properly and our vibrations go down into Decreasing Space, symptoms of "Depression" appear one by one, affecting our lives in many ways. Or, if by other circumstances, we *over* activate our vibrations up into Increasing Space, different stages of "Stress" will be faced that are equally harmful for balancing our beings. (See graphic No. 8)

Graphic No. 8

DEPRESSION   STRESS

Whichever the case, the more we move away from our *Middle, Optimal, or Original Point* of frequency, the more our body, mind, and spirit lose connection with the primary sources.

When we go far from the Optimal Point of frequency, our nature dissipates and becomes deformed. The positive forces decrease; the real transform into something unreal. And if the vibrations reach our own Frequential Field edge of either side, our raw material will be forced to take the last step of simply stop being.

I want to emphasize this: "If we don't stimulate our energy to a suitable degree, we will be out of tune and *depressed*. And, if we stimulate our energy disproportionally, we will also go out of tune and *stressed*."

In this book I just focus on depressive stages, because all the material related to *stress* is a subject for another publication.

Vibrating in Decreasing Space

All our Frequential Space mini-spectrum is composed by hundreds of levels. Each one of these levels generates a different condition and emotion to us. Using the decimal scale as a reference, let's say the center of our body is level number 10, which handles the highest frequency inside the Decreasing Space. Going down in the range, number 9 through number 1 are assigned correspondingly to lower levels, until number 0 where the field ends. (See graphic No. 9)

Graphic No. 9

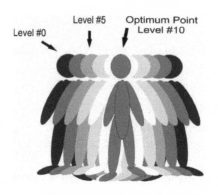

When we are in tune, 100% of life positive aspects vibrate at level number 10. All information necessary for our body to self-building and maintain its good operation, all true thoughts that produce pleasant emotions, and all altruistic concepts that allow self-growth are available gifts for us if our energy keeps the frequency at this level number 10.

But with each step we go away from the tune point, a positive aspect is lost and the opposite negative aspect is gained; at each diminished degree of energy, a constructive element disappears and a destructive one takes life.

In level number 9, we live 90% of positive aspects and begin to experience 10% of negatives. In stage number 8, we tune 80% of positive aspects and gain 20% of negatives. And, thus, we continue in a proportional count down, until arriving at number 0 where we completely lose the capacity to feel any positive vibration, and catch 100% of negative ones.

For example, if my body frequency is kept in level number 7, only 70% of correct energy will flow through me, and the rest will be out of tune. I will have an acceptable physical condition, but sooner or later, those parts of my body that are out of the right vibration will begin to fail. Or if my frequency stays in number 3, I will feel heavy and weak all the time; only 30% of my body parts will respond properly, and the rest will progressively lose their correct operational capacities.

Something similar happens with Mental Energy. If my brain frequency is at number 8, 20% of the information will be lost and my emotions will be slightly negative. Or if I drop my mind to a much lower state like number 2, 80% of my thoughts will appear confused and distorted, bringing devastating feelings constantly.

The same process occurs with the Spiritual Energy.

Depending on the amount of vibration given to our energy currents, we will feel the intensity of their benefits. The proximity to Optimal Point of frequency is *directly proportional* to favorable, healthy, and useful conditions; but the distance from this midpoint, is *inversely proportional* to them.

So we may say depressive states appear when Physical, Mental, and Spiritual energies vibrate at any frequency *below* number 10. And according to the position at which we remain in the Decreasing Space, different personal characteristics will be noticeable.

Let me show a general perspective: usually many people keep their vibrations at not-so-low levels (for example number 9 or number 8) and believe the few negative aspects that manifest are an integral part of their personalities. They are individuals who, although not mired in sadness, barely laugh. They have enough energy to carry out normal responsibilities, however, their bodies feel heavy and dislike physical activity; and even if they seem healthy, are vulnerable to illness. They get used to living with a little of emptiness... a little of bitterness... a little of pain.

For people who usually vibrate at numbers like 6 or 7, discomfort and affliction is normal; presenting neuralgias and chronic pains. They develop unsociable, pessimistic, and irritable temperaments; handling insecurity and low self-esteem. They feel uncomfortable with changes and new adventures... they feel victims of the world.

In levels like numbers 4 or 3, stronger symptoms begin to manifest. People lose desire to do any type of physical activity. Sadness and anguish remain. The senses fall asleep. It is almost impossible to maintain a good performance in relationships or work. Also, self- rejection and an inclination for dying appear.

In lower planes, as numbers 2 or 1, individuals remain asleep for long periods of time, coordination fails and body movement is almost impossible. They exhibit total disinterest towards normal dynamics and responsibilities. There is no desire for eating, listening, or speaking.... there is no desire even to be touched. The negative situation becomes too overwhelming that impulse to take the own life increases.

At last step, number 0, the contact with life's source is almost exhausted. The agony and desperation are inconceivable. There is not a bit of desire, sense, or hope. States outside reality are experienced, in which everything is perceived cloudy and turbulent. And a strong force appears to be preventing the person from continuing… from existing.

Unfortunately, farther we move away from the attraction energy produced by the core of our being, less connection we have with life. And if we go below level number 0 all bonds that unite us to the Essential Energy are lost; passing into another state of frequency, out our rank of existence.

Depression

Remember, we are born *in tune* and natural instinct urges us to stimulate our energy. But as we grow, negative situations, unhealthy habits, and inappropriate conditions have to be faced; changing our vibrational level and pushing us to experience low frequency sensations out of our connection range.

Inadequate life habits of diet, exercise, and resting; harmful practices like drinking, smoking, or drug use; and other conditions as noise, contamination, and pollution have caused many of us to poorly stimulate our body or uncontrollably overload it, carrying the Physical Energy beyond its balance point.

Closed and radical religions; overcrowded environments that generate deficient education systems, social problems, and arbitrary events; devastating and sensationalist news focus by the media; and others, generally push us to think and feel in negative. We sentence our Mental Energy to be out of tune, and, sadly, we create a habit of it.

And keeping our mind far from its Optimal Point reduces the possibility to make contact with higher energies of wisdom, to generate positive changes, and to elevate our spirit; darkening the transformational miracles offered by the Spiritual Energy.

For this reason, most of the time, it is so difficult to have a good life performance. We lose self-security and don't manage to take correct pathways that will give us happiness. We assume mistaken approaches with our kids, choose inappropriate people to share with, and embrace careers that don't fulfill our personal expectations. We create pain, confusing thoughts, unhealthy emotions, problems, and sufferings that are not required for our evolution. We feel incapable of taking control of our own destiny.

Yes! We are definitively surrounded by infinite aspects that throw our vital energy into depressive states, placing us in a world that lacks logic or sense.

Later chapters will explain how each of the three primary currents works, what happens when they are out of balance, and how they can be stimulated to recover their correct flow.

For now, let's conclude:

"Depression is generated when personal energy vibrates in Decreasing Space frequencies; and gradually, some or all of the physical, mental, and spiritual components necessary to maintain an ideal development are lost."

Memories of My Experience...

Honestly, it is very difficult to explain how I felt during this period of my journey. Too much information had arrived in my head and needed to be understood. Nevertheless, everything began to make sense, convincing me that definitely I was neither crazy nor ill as I had been told.

For some reason, in the course of growing, my three energies left the Optimal Frequency I had when I was young. Being in the interference levels became a habit, preventing me from seeing and feeling life clearly.

Thus, insecurity only occurred when I blocked security; I was seized by fear just when tranquility flow was cut; and sadness marked me when I shadowed the joy. My vital currents were out of sync... my light was extinguished... my internal fire was consumed.

But I realized that complicated steps or too much work were *not* required to balance my three primary currents. Only simple, normal, and innate tools of my nature had to be rescued, which would stimulate and maintain my energy into a correct place of vibration.

The first requirement for recovering *my raw material original state* was to have a deep and sincere conviction for changing. Fortunately, I was willing to place the *batteries* into my *radio* and listen to the assigned stations; to open the windows of my being, so a new breeze could enter and refresh my body, mind, and spirit; to leave the past behind and undertake the present that would generate a different future ahead.

The second condition was to adopt correct habits and behaviors, for my essential energies to accommodate. This way I could:

- Develop a much more resistant body and improve my health.
- Reprogram my mind to hold positive thinking, and remain open to talent, creativity, and logic.
- Create a favorable atmosphere where the spiritual current could fit, elevate, and awake my conscience.

And third, I had to accept that feeling *well* was an entirely personal task of perseverance and dedication, with absolute effectiveness. That it did not matter how much I wracked my brain trying to find those "responsible" for my imbalance and immobility; or how much I continued fighting the outside circumstances, feeling a victim of this "evil world" and its "wickedness"; because I will always find not just one, but tens, hundreds, or thousands of elements on which the weight and guilt of this situation could be placed... a situation that, definitively, was in my hands to transform.

I decided not to focus on problems, but on solutions. Exploring different methods how to stimulate my Physical, Mental, and Spiritual Energies, one by one, I would be able to exchange many of my old habits for more effective ones to unblock myself.

In this stage I understood to make real changes and obtain happiness was so much easier of what I had thought. If the Universal Energy was a source of just positive aspects, and when I move away from it, the negative ones come; then the only thing to do was take practical measures, letting the essence flow that connect me… that tune me. The rest would be in the universe's hands!

As when my body is oxygenated and activated while rhythmically breathing, I enjoy the benefits of air without even being conscious of the process. But if my nose and mouth are covered with a very tight bandage, soon my body reacts anxiously. I feel distressed and fight to breathe; I go out of control, more and more, as my breath is exhausted. When the only thing I have to do is remove the bandage, give a great sigh, and let the air do its work. What can be easier?

Thus, I finally started the exciting journey of recovering one of the gifts from God: the base of our material expression… the First Original Current… *the Physical Energy…*

X
Our
Physical Energy

The Material Energy is the prime or basic substance that supports the whole universe; a "red cloud" that gives origin not just to our bodies and our entire physical world, but also to the rest of perceivable elements across the cosmos.

In the moment we are conceived, a *portal* or *window* is opened in a specific place of the universal spectrum. Immediately increasing vibrations connect with emissions transmitted by the Material Current, generating a channel through which the raw material and necessary information to build our body –with characteristics maybe similar but never equal to another being– are captured.

The magnificent universe gives us a beautiful and perfectly coordinated physical device, equipped with sufficient components to delight us with infinite sensations and to survive the space and time adventure.

Our Physical Energy at its Optimal Point

After the fertilization "spark," and thanks to mother's direct stimulation, our energy gradually increases its vibration. Thus, some body part manifests at each level of frequency through a progressive process, until all the corporal range is complete.

Cell by cell, tissue to tissue, muscle after muscle, organ by organ appear smoothly and delicately, before reaching the Optimal Point of frequency assigned for each one of us in the spectrum.

Like an apple tree that, thanks to solar light and earth nutrients excitation, at certain part of its branches begins to increase the vibration. So one small green fruit is created, which grows as vibration increases. Not only does its size change, but also its color; from the *green* frequency, it rises to the *red* frequency. Also its skin begins to shine, its interior goes from hard to soft, and its flavor turns from bitter to sweet; until the apple reaches a point where it is *ripe* and in excellent condition to be consumed.

Likewise, when we manage to tune our Physical Energy to the correct frequency, all the corporal pieces acquire essential data to work at one hundred percent (100%). Heart, brain, lungs, and every other organ offer their particular service in an effective way. The blood along with all chemicals and fluids run with suitable speed and volume. The senses are completely activated; eyes, ears, mouth, nose, and skin are ready to react to any environmental agent our body detects. The skin appears fresh, the hair shiny, and nails and teeth solid. The corporal weight keeps proportionate, facilitating mobility and flexibility.

Maintaining our exact frequency of vibration creates a general state of vigor, effectiveness, and balance. We feel alive and may run, jump, dance, and sing. There is neither a pain nor slowness; only well-being and freedom. We radiate an aspect of vitality, health, and beauty.

Our Physical Energy in Decreasing Space Levels or Frequential Depression

I want my dear reader to pay close attention to the following paragraph: *"All elements in nature tend to lower, slowly and progressively, the internal vibrations of their own matter, if they are not activated by some external stimulus that maintains its frequency in Optimal Point."*

If the *apple tree* example is again used, and this question is raised: "What would happen if the juicy fruit is taken from the branch and left for many days outdoors on the ground?" We will find that without activation provided by the tree's nutrients, the apple essential particles vibrations begin to decrease.

Little by little, its skin texture becomes wrinkled; the flavor goes from sweet to acidic; the color loses its brightness, fading to brown tones; the shape becomes deformed. And it arrives to a so low oscillation speed that ends up rotting, and organisms able to develop in low frequencies –like insects and bacteria– start to consume it.

The general aspect of *agreeable and healthy* results in *disagreeable and unhealthy!*

Analogously, at birth we lose the direct support offered by our mother, and later in life if our body is not activated in effective means, the internal vibrations will progressively decline. One after another, each body part slows its own oscillations, damaging the functionality in an opposite sequence to which it was manifested.

The organism that was built in an increasing succession starts to deteriorate in a decreasing way. Organ by organ, muscle after muscle, tissue to tissue, cell by cell go out of tune and get *un-programmed*; exhibiting opposite conditions to those that gave them life.

When activation is incorrect, our body feels heavy and loses mobility. Muscles become flaccid. Joints stiffen –like never opened door hinges– and pains and neuralgias increase. Appetite is lost and corporal weight is drastically altered, changing the natural and aesthetic figure. Skin becomes opaque and withered; our aspect is perceived as haggard. Hair loses its natural brightness and mobility. Glands fail to produce indispensable hormones for a good physical performance. Heart lowers its power and diminishes the blood pressure necessary to properly irrigate the entire body. Internal PH begins to change from alkaline to acidic.

As vibrations diminish, our capacity to enjoy the sensations offered by the world around also decreases. Our senses more easily perceive negative impulses than positive ones: we see ugly when pretty; we taste bitter when sweet; and the touch of any hand no longer causes pleasure, but revulsion.

When very low vibration levels are reached, microorganisms of low frequency such as bacteria and viruses come alive, developing infections or diseases that sometimes can be devastating. Also the brain fails to process the Mental Energy accurately.

In general, the corporal balance and coordination start to collapse. And all those thousands processes that have occurred for the creation of our physical matter, go back in an inverse way, bringing harmful health conditions.

Our body little by little stops being a body, and the adventure of living begins to lose its enchantment!

Always remember, our physical body must constantly have a specific impulse *equal* to the frequency assigned to us when we are born; a generator, a battery, or an electrical current producing the necessary energy to keep the radio in tune. Otherwise, we fall into the Frequential Decreasing Space and start to leave our assigned place on the great cosmic scale.

How can we stimulate our Physical Energy and maintain its Optimal Point of Frequency?

So often we are looking for *magical* solutions that provide immediate well-being, and mistakenly we clutch to expensive medicines, artificial products, stimulant substances, complicated dynamics, or turn to other people who promise "miracles" for fixing our ailments.

However, we are the *magicians,* and the real methods to remain healthy are in our hands. The key elements for ensuring balance are generally found in front of our noses, but we don't see them… we don't hear them… we don't use them… we don't enjoy them. Maybe because they seem so simple, natural, and perhaps ordinary, we doubt about their value to transform us into what we really are: simple and natural.

Let's see some of the most important and essential aspects for harmonizing Physical Energy:

a) MOVEMENT: How easy and normal it is to move the body? Movement is the first human instinct and a requirement to stay alive. It is the basic force or generator that allows the physical *machine* to convert mechanical energy into electromagnetic energy; producing the right power flow to maintain our being in tune with the Material Current.

The amount of *action* we have at a certain time, will determinate the frequency of our body during this same time. Thus, little or no-movement forces us to remain vibrating in Decreasing Space levels, and extreme action makes us exceed the midpoint and enter to vibrate in Increasing Space levels. This is why it is so important to move in a *constant, balanced, and completely rhythmical* way; always trying to keep the correct Optimal Point vibration.

People with sedentary lifestyle, staying at a single site without much change to exercise, are most likely to become physically ill and present depressive states –even slightly. The body parts which are poorly activated are the first to display negative conditions, and the lower our body power load goes... the lower our emotions fall.

Today the importance of exercise is widely promoted. So, with desire to lose weight or feel "very healthy," people mistakenly turn to the opposite side and over-load their bodies with too much energy; also going out of balance.
Don't forget that excessive body stimulation can be as harmful as poor stimulation.

Then it is necessary to look for sports or joyful physical dynamics that can be done in moderation. More specifically, coordinated movements involving all corporal zones where energy may proportionally arrive to each corner of the body; but they cannot be abrupt or debilitating, and under any circumstance cause pain.

Based on this, I want to highlight two activities that, for me, are the most complete, harmonic, natural, and pleasant: dancing and swimming.

- *Dancing.* Unfortunately dancing has lost through history not just its basic structure, but its true function for helping our body well-being. In so many cultures, dancing is disappearing, and in others, it has been transformed exclusively for entertainment, loaded with difficult-to-learn techniques executed by select groups.

But the authentic objective when moving our "skeleton" is to produce permanent and rhythmical energetic excitation that maintains all the organism's pieces in their optimal frequencies. Dance offers the possibility of executing movements inherent to our corporal design in smooth and coordinated way, and it allows us to freely enjoy self-expression and a tensionless interaction with space. In addition, the vibrations generated by musical sound waves, combined with other beneficial elements such as socialization and joy offered by group dance, create a result difficult to exceed by any other type of physical exercise.

Dance was born with human race and we cannot let it die. Let's enjoy happy rhythms and feel no fear when moving our heads, shoulders, arms, hips, legs, and any other muscle. It doesn't matter if we are kids, adults, or seniors; men or women; single, couple, or group; if we are in a ballroom, living room, or park. Just dance!

- *Swimming.* This activity is part of our instincts too. Not it only stimulates all our body parts with ordered, symmetrical, and regular movements, but it forces us to breathe deeply. It should be practiced frequently and smoothly.

Just think about the benefits of swimming in the sea, where stimulating aspects like movement, water, sun, salt, wind, and sand join in a mixture beyond excellence!

I also recommend *Walking*, which is, without a doubt, the base of our movement. The impact of the feet hitting the ground activates all nerve endings located in the soles and ignites the rest of our nerve system. However, for more effectiveness, it should be complemented with neck, shoulders, arms, back, and hips stimulation.

Always remember, the dynamism was sent to us like a great tool to be enjoyed, but *not* to torture our bodies. And whatever we choose to do –Yoga, Tai Chi, Pilates, Zumba, gardening, or juggling– we must express ourselves freely and be replenished by the invigorating force of any action.

b) OXYGEN: The universe is so perfect that it makes *vitality* available to us only by way of an aspiration. The oxygen in air is pure energy in a gaseous state and its high vibration level intensifies everything that comes into contact with it. We must get the habit to inhale and exhale in an appropriate and precise way, so the total of our organism can be stimulated.

There are hundreds of techniques promoting the great benefits of the simple, natural, and ordinary act of breathing, and we must adopt any of them as an important lifestyle.

Keep in mind that a good *inspiration* can be hundred times more productive than other stimulants.

c) SUNLIGHT: The powerful waves of light and heat produced by the *sun* are essential and irreplaceable to our physical system. The more solar radiation, the higher our vibrations; the less radiation, the less our matter is excited.

Our corporal frequency changes by day hours. Noon offers greater stimulus than early morning or late afternoon, and during night the corporal vibration naturally goes down when our "smiling yellow fellow" incentive is absent.

In the same way, lack of solar rays for prolonged periods of time can affect us greatly. For example, people who stay indoors without having direct contact with sun –due to work or other conditions– are prone to depress their energy and enter into negative physical and emotional states. Or in those countries that face long winters, without sufficient sunlight stimulation, inhabitants commonly present depressive symptoms.

In hot times, mood rises; in cold times, mood lowers.

The sun is one of the most powerful energy activators and must be received on daily basis. But although we cannot be deprived of its vivifying benefits, neither should we exceed to its exposure because it may also bring harmful consequences.

Let's use this *shining universal gift* responsibly and wisely.

d) WATER: We often hear about the importance of drinking a good amount of water to maintain health, and this recommendation should not be taken for granted!

This irreplaceable "liquid gift" not only makes up 70 to 85 percent of our body, but it is also the most efficient compound for transporting energy. It is well known as a *conductive element*, which facilitates circulation of all nutrients and fluids essential for life, and also expels toxins.

Let's maintain a good-hydration habit, especially in early morning before digesting any food. However, don't forget to regulate its consumption too.

Excessive water in a healthy organism can knock it out of balance, and a shortage of water may restrain our vigor... may stop our life.

e) NATURAL ELEMENTS: Every element of the material world produces a unique and exclusive impulse to each part of our physical body. Foods, plants, minerals, crystals, animals, and all other components of nature can raise or lower our corporal frequency, depending on the vibratory level they are. And according to the intensity in which these stimuli occur, the sensations can be positive or negative for us.

Because this subject is too extensive, next, I am going to highlight just few examples that will at least provide a general concept of how this works.

If something exists that definitely influences the good or bad condition of human body it is the *food* range. Unfortunately, diet is another field that has been distorted in most, not to say all, cultures of our history. We feed ourselves unconsciously, unaware of what foods raise or lower our vibrations; which consumables are appropriate for our age, life style, day time, or climate of the region we live.

All this has led the majority of people to change their body's original frequency and get used to vibrate in Frequential Spaces; being permanently affected by *diseases and ailments*.

The benefits of foods can vary according to how and when are used. If our body is low energy, we should consume high vibration products for stimulation and balance. On the contrary, if we are over-stimulated and our energy is vibrating in a very high degree, it is better to look for low-load nutrients that degrade our frequency.

For example, consuming a high vibration substance such coffee may generate a stimulating effect to *inactive* people, but it can harmfully exceed the energy of those *hyperactive* ones. In addition, the caffeine effect is stronger during noon when our internal energy waves are already high, than during morning hours, when the body is still at rest. Many goods –like industrial sugars, flours, fats, processed foods, or red wine– may lower our energy and make already-depressive people feel worse; on the other hand those goods may calm the anxiety of over-stimulated and stressed people.

Fortunately, ancient philosophies that use food as well-being agents are now being recovered. According to different ideologies, foods can be classified as yin or yang, cold or warm, high or low calories, those that expand energy and those that contract it. Also are classified according to their color and flavor frequency, and recommended based on the day time, season, or temperature in the moment of eating. Equally important is a proper food identification and combination.

Diet and corporal cycles alignment is an art that we all must learn, in the interest not only to our matter good performance, but also to stabilize our emotional state. We should always keep our frequency in its Optimal Point; otherwise, we will continue being prisoners of diseases, pain, and toxic conditions that may obstruct our welfare.

Now, similarly, we can continue discovering the reactions of our body when making contact with elements like scents, colors, textures... with light, water, fire, air, earth.

For example:

- If we want to boost our body energy it is better to wear white or light-color clothes, and if we want to decrease our frequency rather use black or dark tones.

Organic materials like wool, silk, or cotton generate more vibrations than synthetic ones.

- Staying in touch with living beings such as trees, flowers, plants, and domestic animals can be very helpful for raising our environmental and corporal energy.

- Walking barefoot on the ground, grass, or sand incites much more energy to feet nerve endings than wearing shoes with insulated soles like rubber.

- Crystals and minerals are compounds that Mother Nature charges as *batteries*; offering a wide and amazing spectrum of stimuli. But we must look for those that appropriately balance our energy and avoid the ones that may cause annoying interferences.

- A room painted with a cold color as "green apple" spreads a tranquil and restful sensation, but a hot tone like "red fire" produces much more excitement.

- And we cannot forget some of the grandmothers' recipes! Like the use of a *cold* ice cube (low oscillation substance) to calm the extreme vibration of a skin burn, or a *hot* cup of tea to relax the tension produced by a stomach cramp.

Anyway, there is plenty information for those wishing to extend this subject, especially in the internet. Material about *therapeutic* uses of aromas, colors, oils, rays of light; crystals as healing agents; homemade natural remedies; and others offering a practical, entertaining, and, I would say, efficient knowledge in how to stabilize our energies.

The "bad state of health" is a situation that we humans have generated because of our incorrect way of eating and drinking, and the poor interaction with the rest of the wonderful natural tools. I want to emphasize the following: *"Poor health is not a requirement of our destiny and much less a test sent by God for humans to learn lessons."*

We most please our senses, acquire good habits of life, and get the real benefit from this other part of the great *celestial legacy*.

f) MUSIC and SINGING: Like dancing, these two activities have been part of humanity since its beginning, and are other pleasant forms of stimulation.

Our body is considerably activated when we sing, because the vocal cords generate internal waves with the intensity dictated by our "vigorous lungs." In addition, the vibratory waves produced by sound, of a huge variety of musical instruments, can neutralize our energy currents at any moment.

Let's listen to smooth music when want to calm our matter, or enjoy energetic rhythms with high vibrations –like those of drums– if we feel down and wish to reactivate our being. And do not forget the joy and excitement certain tunes may bring when we match their lyrics with our pleasant memories.

Rhythmic and harmonic frequencies are the language that allows us to be in tune with the rest of the universe. So even if we have a "trembling" voice, we must sing and let exhilarating melodies touch and elevate our souls.

g) LAUGHING: Another charming tool used to accelerate our material essence. This peculiar action that combines the thoracic box, throat, and lungs, creates rhythmical vibrations, which highly raise body frequency. Plus the benefit we obtain from the great amount of air inhaled at the moment of a *big guffaw.*

Remember, *laugher* can be carried everywhere without taking up space; it doesn't need manual to be activated; and we can enjoy it alone or accompanied. Best of all, laughing can be acquired freely; although it is possible to use particular aids like "Laughter Therapy" in which directed sessions are offered.

There are many reasons for crying, but let's choose those that make us laugh... those that make us thrill.

h) RELATIONSHIPS: Intimate gestures as caresses, kisses, hugs, or a good body massage have a quite stimulating effect, because not only they push the nervous system and heart to flow harder, but also the vibrations produced by two or more people are unified.

For example, *sexuality* is one of human being natural activities that boost our frequencies further, and lead us to experience maximal well-being, "even only for few seconds." No wonder why many ancestral cultures –like the Chinese– consider sexuality *an art* that assures health and longevity.

Let loving, cheerful, respectful, and positive people share their energy with us.

Well! I could continue naming various aspects that influence the way in which we vibrate, but it is difficult to cover all of them. Nevertheless, remember, the physical body is temporary home of our *being* and it was designed with greatest degree of excellence. And keeping it in good condition offers us the possibility of tasting freedom of movement, of action... freedom of sensations, of pleasures... freedom of existence. Everything is in our hands.

Finally, I need to point out that a balanced Physical Energy is the only *admission ticket* to tune the Mental Energy; and, consequently, it will be the only *pass* to connect us with the Spiritual Energy. In the same way the development of our three essential currents successively appeared, they will decay one by one in an inverse manner when the base of everything –the physical organism– is unstable.

If the energy is extinguishing, our body will be exhausting; if the body is exhausting, our mind will be disconnecting; and if the mind is disconnecting, our spirit will be dying.

"Life is like a game of managing vibrations that gives us the privilege of feeling through the wonderful *physical shell* the infinite universal spectrum. And keeping ourselves stimulated, will offer us a body worthy of housing a shining mind and an exalted spirit."

Memories of My Experience...

In this wonderful stage, I would remember something my younger brother frequently repeated to me:

- "Patricia, *exercise* will get rid of all your aches!"

But with so much frustration, I thought:

- "I am too skinny to go to a gym; I will probably disappear! And besides, what movement has to do with my emotions?"

Luckily, later, I understood that in order to continue forward, my body had to be stimulated. It would be very difficult, because exercising was neither my habit nor my great pleasure. However, if for many years I had the will to take antidepressant pills daily, then *movement* would have to be part of my basic needs... part of my medicine.

I wrote a list of joyful activities, and, definitively, dancing was on top. Few were the opportunities I had in life for dancing and singing, but I remembered the indescribable pleasure it was. And considering *parties* were still limited, I simply decided to dance with myself. It seemed pretty crazy, but it didn't matter; I just was determined to be a "possibly nutty, but happy" person.

I looked at home for an open and comfortable place for exercising. With happy music, I developed a dynamic that allowed me to move all my body parts freely –head, neck, shoulders, arms, hip, trunk, legs, and feet– and it was complemented with different breathing techniques.

In the beginning, my body didn't respond well because its stiffness and little flexibility. So I initiated with a short routine (five or ten minutes) and later went for longer time (thirty or fifty minutes.)

Amazingly, soon, the changes were reconstructive! I acquired agility and skill; my physical discomforts started to disappear; my body felt less heavy, having more energy to continue daily chores; I found the desire to play with my children and go anywhere; and my senses awoke with emotion to enjoy everything that in the past stimulated me during my childhood.

Besides the movement program, I tried to do every day, or at least three or four times a week, I decided to assume *housework* as complement and have an organized and pleasant atmosphere that encouraged everyone in the family. Surely if somebody had peeked through the window, they would laugh looking at the amusing *dance* sessions I began having with my new partners "the broom and duster." The acts of sweeping, cleaning, washing, and organizing stopped being a reason for me to feel abused by life; rather, I used them for cheering my life. Also, I acquired other habits such as massaging my feet, hands, and scalp; spending more time in the sun; seeking for opportunities to swim; and paying more attention to diet.

I have to confess, it was easier than I would imagined. As soon as the body energy frequency changed due to movement, my *tastes* also did. I didn't have to push myself, as before, to consume natural foods. My apathy toward products like fats, meats, sodas or alcoholic drinks grew. In addition, suddenly I began to reject smoking, which helped me to stop this bad habit definitively. The enjoyment for open and illuminated spaces gently appeared; without forgetting that my closet was renewed with bright and cheerful color clothes. Not only did my body respond positively, feeling healthy and fortified, but I also perceived myself calm, enthusiastic, and less anxious.

I understood everybody has to be stimulated differently, and we must establish our own habits and speed for maintaining the Optimal Point of energy. Thus, I decided to adopt actions that I like, and with appropriate time and perseverance, they would make me feel comfortable.

Creating new habits is a big process because we tend to return to *bad practices* that have been used for many years. On several occasions, I lost continuity in my exercise routine and immediately fell into old states of fatigue and irritability. However, when thinking about the importance of *movement*, my soul found the strength to do it again.

"Rescuing the grand value of my dear brother's words."

Yes! Without a doubt, my great metamorphosis began when I decided to move and activate my physical body. As always, I am so thankful to the universe for having given me the understanding to *spoil myself* in a pleasant, simple, and natural form; and why not to say it, free of charge.

Fortifying my Physical Energy ended many damaging aspects that were part of me for so long, and created a much more solid base to my personal structure. But, although this was one of my greater earnings, I had to keep strong and continue knocking down the levee that was blocking the base of our mental expression... the Second Original Current... *the Mental Energy...*

XI
Our
Mental Energy

The Mental Energy is the universal current that offers us –evolutionary living beings– the necessary raw material for developing ideas and concepts about our physical experiences. In addition, it is the generator of our emotions.

After birth, with external stimulation, our Physical Energy must continue rising until a certain point of frequency when a *second window* can be opened, allowing the Mental Energy or "yellow mist" to flow.

This is why it is not just until we are a few months old that consciousness is gained, being able to discern our own body and the surroundings. As mental vibrations increase, during growth, we catch more indispensable data for understanding and solving aspects of survival. And constantly we can assimilate additional information that will help our personal development as well as our social progress.

Thanks to the *brain* (high technology material device that serves as a processor or converter) we may perceive *invisible* cosmic waves transmitted by the universal Mental Current. Similar to a computer connected to "Internet"; at the beginning, an initial set of *windows* appear with general guidelines for basic system operation, and later it gives the opportunity to search and *download* any program we want to explore.

Knowledge has always been in the universe. Absolutely all information concerning the complicated subject of existence is inscribed in the Mental Circuit. Past, present, and future are available any moment we get in tune with this magnificent *celestial* memory.

Throughout history, the great geniuses who brought concepts forward by hundreds of years and helped the world's evolution, have somehow maintained a direct link with this powerful energy that manifests in their curious minds.

It is mistaken thinking that the only way to *learn* about all aspects of life is through teachings left by our predecessors. We cannot deny it is testimony of the material that has been previously processed; however, we must understand that when we are correctly connected with the *original mental flow,* we open a channel to assimilate new, advanced, and more-developed judgments. And of course this is also another free gift offered by the Creator.

Knowledge cannot be invented; it can only be picked up, processed, and interpreted. And creativity is not exclusive to the most studied ones, but to those who are most *in tune*!

Now, in addition of being the intellect's basic substance, the Mental Energy is also producer of our *emotions*. Yes! Believe it or not, it is the Mental

Current which generates all perceptions as love, joy, security, tranquility, and thousands more.

As radio antennas, each thought we have produces an *individual and particular* vibratory wave, which immediately connects with an analogous frequency transmitted by the Universal Mind. Thus, the brain receives a unique impulse that is reproduced and amplified toward the interior of our physical body, manifesting some emotion.

Just like a piano key when is pressed and an individual sound spreads stimulating our ears; every idea that vibrates in our head touches a "key" in the cosmos, generating an exclusive "tone" to be broadcast for our "radio." In the same way, our vision, hearing, touch, taste, and smell are meant to perceive wide variety of material stimulus (heat, cold, hard, smooth); "thought" is another *sense* that facilitates our understanding of the impressions offered by the majestic Mental Current.

Our Mental Energy at its Optimal Point

The intellect is also constructed in a gradual way, and when our mental flow reaches its Optimal Point of frequency, it obtains one hundred percent (100%) of necessary material to work effectively.

We begin handling *logic*, which helps our intellectual development; we improve creativity, good memory, and capacity for learning; and the great circulation of new concepts generates questions that urge our *curious* nature to find answers and continue advancing.

All these tools are useful for forming clear and optimistic concepts about life and strategies for surviving; as well as for making correct decisions in any aspect that will produce efficiency, achievements, and prosperity.

In addition, keeping a suitable Mental Energy volume offers us the opportunity for feeling invigorating emotions. Not only because we gained self-esteem, confidence, and security when perceiving ourselves as capable of well social functioning; but also when creating positive thoughts, we guarantee a universal answer that makes us feel "good" physically.

The Mental Energy in precise place of vibration, brings essential conditions for our body, our reason, and, definitively, our heart.

Our Mental Energy in Decreasing Space Levels or Frequential Depression

Just as when physical matter is *low* stimulated, also Mental Energy vibratory speed decreases if we do not urge it to remain in its mid or Optimal Point of Frequency.

As the mind progressively began catching necessary information for handling the body, understanding the environment, and generating ways for surviving; inversely, the data will be gradually erased as the "yellow matter" diminishes its flow.

The *software* that one day constructed our intellect starts to be de-programmed, and the "thought network" begins to fail.

When we are out of tune, ideas become unclear and concepts are distorted. Now the use of *logic* is complicated; concentrating and memorizing is more difficult; creativity begins to vanish; we feel incapable of completing home, work or community improvement projects, clinging firmly to established ones; insecurity and fear about change appears. And not only do we lose the capacity to face difficulties, but our mind literally is blocked for solutions, originating sensations of hopelessness and self-rejection.

When vibrating at low frequencies our thoughts become negative whether we want it or not. General judgments are pessimist and discouraging. Consequently, positive emotions *collapse,* being replaced with impatience, irritability, and rage. And the uncomfortable perception of ourselves makes us look around for whom to blame, and adopt conducts of sarcasm, defensiveness, and, often, aggressiveness.

Let me illustrate with an example:

During early morning hours, my daughter and I are sitting at the dining room, with just enough time to eat breakfast and arrive punctually for school and work. Suddenly, my daughter strikes the milk glass with an *involuntary* movement. It rises into the air and then falls strongly, spilling the precious "white" liquid. Our clothes, tablecloth, and floor get soaked and sticky.

If at that moment my mental state is in a *lower* Decreasing Space level, the circumstances become unpleasant: The first concept I generate from the scene is completely negative. I feel irritated, my heart beats quickly and my blood pressure goes up. I look at the girl with inquisitive eyes, because I see her as the cause of an event that for *my mind* is a great problem. Pessimistic thoughts accumulate, like the effort needed to clean the mess and our lateness for leaving. Most probably, without thinking, I yell at my daughter for being so clumsy, and she cry with fearful expression.

The time me cleaning, fighting with the little one who no longer wants to go to school, trying to over organize my look, and feeling victim of life delay our departure. On the way to school I get so angry with people who go *less fast* than we go, and use more of the few remaining minutes fighting with whoever crossed us. Indeed, we arrive at our destinations behind schedule. And surely I answer in an explosive and defensive way when my boss complains about my tardiness.

This chain of adverse events makes me feel worse. My vibrations, which are already low, fall to even lower levels… levels nobody wants to reach.

Now, if my frequency maintains at half way of the Decreasing Space, my reaction is a little less extreme; but still negative:

My concept about what just happened is as a disadvantage, but I also understand that it is not my girl's fault. I *repress* myself avoiding shouting or demonstrating my great anger; nevertheless, I use second intention comments such as "Why is this happening to me? Now I will have trouble at work; but don't worry, it was not your fault." Just thinking about the delay creates anguish and, perhaps, upsets my stomach. The traffic probably is very congested and most traffic lights are red; however, I feel incapable of changing the matter. In effect, when arriving at the office and having no courage to defend myself when my boss points to my lateness, the rage and frustration increase.

One part of me is conscious that this state is incorrect; the other part is not. That is why throughout the day I battle an inner war of feelings against logic. My vibration stays in tension point, and continuously an effort is made to not think what I think... to not feel what I feel.

In contrast, if my Mental Energy frequency is kept in its *Optimal Point*, the situation appears very differently:

All my reactions are natural, positive, and without resistance. It is very probable that after the morning "milk tsunami" I have a great outburst of laughter and my little one too. Happy ideas spontaneously appear, such as having a "milk war" and a competition to see who cleans and changes clothing first. My girl moves faster than ever, and we are ready in just minutes. Although it seems unbelievable, surely the traffic flows and gets green lights at most intersections. My daughter remains happy in her school. And after arriving "on time", and instead of receiving a reprimand at work, I share with colleagues the stimulating morning I just had.

My body feels well... my mind open ... and my energy vital.

In conclusion, the problem is not that my daughter spilled the milk; the *problem* depends on the level of vibration I am when facing the situation. The lower the Mental Energy vibration goes into Frequential Space, the more our understanding becomes cloudier and our emotional state gets disfigured. The personality dims with conditions that are not part of our essence such as anxiety, distress, desperation, bitterness, sadness, and hopelessness.

Correct thoughts and emotions disappeared, and, lamentably, incorrect ones become a custom... a habit... a lifestyle.

How can we stimulate our Mental Energy and maintain its Optimal Point of Frequency?

Today is well known the importance of taking care of the body, but often we forget the *brain* also has to be "adjusted" constantly.

As well as we take care of our physical self, keeping our mind in an appropriate frequency requires enjoyable conducts and activities that become habit. And again, they might seem simple and too common; however remember behaviors innate to our nature are the most effective... the most productive.

I must emphasize the importance of not overloading our energy, because we will enter the *Stress* field that also generates harmful conditions for mental and emotional stability.

Now, let me review some very important and indispensable aspects to activate the Mental Energy:

a) PHYSICAL ENERGY in BALANCE: As I have mentioned, each one of the three energy currents is independent but at the same time, they are correlated. For this reason when our Physical Energy loses too much frequency, it drags our Mental Current to vibrate in its own Frequential Space.

Keeping a healthy and active *body* facilitates our *mind* tuning; otherwise we have to make double effort to conserve a favorable mental process. (Ways to stimulate the Physical Energy can be found in the preceding chapter)

b) POSITIVE THOUGHTS: The act of reasoning positively is part of our congenital characteristics, and is available from the first moment our Mental Current enters to flow in the brain during early childhood.

Unfortunately, in a world as confused as ours, affirmative thinking is very difficult to maintain; due to many aspects that push our rational flow toward negative spaces, inducing us to habits that keep our vibrations out of tune. But, resuming and activating the initial attitude of the intellect is easier than we thought. Today diverse systems of how to recover thinking positive are available. A large amount of books, videos, and CDs promoting self-growing and mental control can be found in bookstores, libraries, internet, and other sites. We can choose whatever offers us comfort, pleasure, and, mainly, good results.

Even though, I want to comment on an activity that, for me, has the greatest degree of effectiveness when trying mind optimization: "meditation."

- *Meditation* is a term used for many different techniques –practiced worldwide– that produce brain vibrations analogous to those emitted by the great Universal Mental Current.

Throughout history most cultures have created their *own* disciplines of concentration and self-gathering, trying to focus thoughts and harmonize whole being. And even the majority of these methods are so effective, later I will present one I developed and which helped me to change my life forever: "Radio-Meditation."

Meanwhile, I may say *meditation* is the *Gym* to maintain mind's good shape; and if it is included as part of our daily routine, like eating or dressing, it can be one of the most powerful instruments for amazing personal transformations. I recommend meditation practice in calm and natural sites like beaches, gardens, or parks. Although, most favorable is a reserved comfortable place in our home; letting know everybody that it is our "sacred spot" and we shouldn't be interrupted while we are there.

Body relaxation and contemplation on something particular such as objects, images, sensations, or simply emptiness, can take our brain *back* to vibrate at its original and pleasant frequency. If we project vibrations of wisdom, we will obtain wise answers; if we think about happiness, joy instead of sadness we will perceive; if we visualize peace, peace we will feel. And if the desire is to experience any positive *noun* that can be found in the dictionary (security, patience, strength, optimism, tolerance or pardon) exactly these emotions will be part of us thanks to meditation.

Thinking positively makes us participants of the goodness that existence offers... thinking negatively will transform us into accomplices of confusion, obstruction, suffering, and distance from who we really are.

c) LOGIC: It is the ability to make right decisions and act effectively when we want to obtain a specific result. It is another innate tool of our species that aids us to create mental vibrations equal to those from Mental Energy.

Hundreds of pleasant activities –many left behind by modern times– promote attention focusing on a mechanical process. Urging not only our ability to observe, concentrate, discern, and construct in a *logical* form; but generally may be key elements for us to socialize with family, relatives, and friends.

Some of those activities are:

- Put together puzzles
- Complete crosswords
- Sew, embroider, or knit
- Make handcrafts with any type of material such as ceramic, glass, wood, paper, etc.
- Play board games like chess or cards
- Build or assemble toys
- Complete mathematical or numerical activities
- Memorize poems, tongue-twisters, or riddles
- Read aloud

Or whatever ingenious function that pushes our "noodle" to work.

The universe is logical, coordinated, exact, precise. And the frequent use of *reasoning* brings us *in tune* with these valuable attributes.

d) DRAWING, PAINTING and SCULPTURE: Visual arts that are also part of humanity's universal legacy.

The process of observing, designing, and constructing any project that conjugates lines, forms, composition, and balance, not only allows us to develop self-expression and obtain a visible result, but it also generates very favorable level brain vibrations.

Let's develop the ability to diffuse charcoal on virgin spaces to give our thoughts an image... let's play with textures, materials, and colors to express what our heart yearns for... let's be delighted by the scene view where existence is developed: *beauty*.

Could anything be more pleasant and recreational?

e) PLAYING MUSICAL INSTRUMENTS: The action of transmitting music through manual *devices* is an ancient human inclination.

The logical and coordinated process that different parts of our body need for activating an instrument, along with the sound waves emitted by it, may stimulate our brain greatly and change our frequency for good.

Playing any of the thousands instruments that exist around the world, combined with singing and dancing if possible, can become a much more effective "remedy" than any medication.
Choosing whichever, definitely will serve as therapy to concentrate our mind and enchant our soul.

f) WRITING: Printing signs or symbols by hand in a rational and uniform way, is another tool has been neglected because seems too normal and current.

Spontaneously writing our thoughts and emotions is the best method for putting ideas in order, clarifying concepts about life, and helping self-knowledge. And it doesn't matter if we are amateur writers; let's write just for elevating our Mental and Emotional Current... let's write for bringing alive the natural instinct that pushes us to transmit our experiences and wisdom through *ink*.

To be able to get connected with the majestic "yellow circuit," we must:

- Desire to vibrate with it.

- Adopt healthy and practical habits that allow channeling our ideas clearly.
- Be open to all information and emotions sent to us.

Every time we want to experience a *true and worthy desire*, some part of the infinite cosmic spectrum flow though us. We don't have to fight irrational and negative feelings; we just have to let logical and positive ones run.

Finally, let's remember that only a *balanced* mind –with right vibrations– permits the Spiritual Energy circulation. And it makes possible the manifestation of that *wise and divine voice,* which speaks within us and patiently waits to be listened.

"Thanks to the wonderful Universal Mind, we are honored of catching information and feeling sensations *beyond* the material world. We are privileged of being conscious of our own existence. And keeping our mind stimulated is an exclusive key that opens the next door for our spiritualization and our evolution as eternal beings."

Memories of My Experience...

I had already taken the first step to stimulate my physical body. But, during this stage, I also understood that practical measures to tune my mental frequency and manage my connection with the correct cosmic transmissions were needed.

I finally accepted, thinking in self-defeating way became my *habit*. And although I felt that reprogramming my brain, which had been set in low vibration levels for so many years, would be almost impossible; I was convinced if *free will* was the "dial" to change my "radio station," then my intense desire to keep going forward would be the engine for obtaining it.

I swear I never imagined how easy is to be *reconnected* with original emissions. Because when thinking about *meditation*, I conjured images of very thin, almost skeletal men, with long gray hair and beards, dressed in a white-linen-diaper shape folded cloth, seated in a "knot" position along the Ganges River, India, or over a "softy" mattress of finishing nails; ancient practices, too eccentric for my culture.

But now that the panorama was clearer, I verified meditation is the most effective instrument for mind tuning, and it is not necessary to use complicated techniques... or have a "rubber" body... or be in strange places... or interminable hours of silence and calm are required. On the contrary, meditation can be done just in few minutes and at familiar places effectively and easily.

So, based on the concept of being organisms that transmit and receive radio waves, I adopted an activity I named "Radio-Meditation." With this simple practice of using *affirmative words*, I urge my intellect to produce only high vibrations and stimulate emotions; driving my Mental Energy to its natural state again.

I found the best moment for concentration and tranquility when, every night, my little daughter asked me to pray at the edge of her bed until she fall asleep.
While my "Sleeping Beauty" was going into her dreams, I managed to relax my body, breathing deeply, and feeling part of the silence. I thought about *lovely* things I wanted to obtain; trying to be very specific in order to receive something in return.

Then, I made a list of words that form the positive spectrum and grouped them according to different aspects of life; creating one *initial or basic* meditation, like this:

-**Mind***: creativity, illumination, understanding, wisdom, clarity, and truth.*

-**Heart:** *love, tranquility, peace, joy, respect, pardon, and kindness.*

-**Spirit:** *security, strength, motivation, honesty, dedication, and integrity.*

-**Body:** *health, vitality, beauty, balance, and excellence.*

-General: *harmony, humor, prosperity, productivity, communication, and accomplishment.*

Adding many other terms that complemented the list, I repeated all words daily. Visualizing the "universal mist" entering through a "window" above my head and transmitting its respective sensations, my mind's energy frequency increased and created a tickly feeling in the rest of my body. It took approximately five or ten minutes; although, if possible, I made it longer.

I know, my dear reader, you are probably asking:

- "This is it?"

And my answer is:

- "Doing it correctly; yes. This is it, for now!"

Because later, the *basic meditation* will be replaced with a more complete one, which also helps tune the Spiritual Energy. And let me say it, if I hadn't experienced this in my own life, I would never believe that something so simple could produce the amazing results were appearing when meditation became part of my necessities.

As vibrating positively, my thoughts appeared optimistic and my emotions pleasant. My perception expanded. My intellect was more lucid for understanding new information. Now I could face situations that created rage and distress with calmness and resolution, turning them into something enriching. And one of the first changes I noticed in my emotional state was when bad mood and sadness yielded patience and joy.

As I became more confident, creative, and wiser in my way of thinking, feeling, speaking, and acting, miraculously the behavior of those who surrounded me also transformed. Thus, the interaction with my children and friends turned warm and open. The relationship with my husband recovered qualities lost over the course of years, and new ones that fortified our marriage were gained.

By reaffirming the inventory of positive words, I created a kind of "energy quake;" a shake-up that effectively moved and rearranged all the elements of my life. Similar to when we have a chessboard and play a strategic game to obtain a skillful result; I did not have to change my "board" to continue playing, I simply adopted different tactics to make the "game" more stimulating.

I felt strange enjoying and feeling a real sense in everything that I made, and watching with optimism circumstances I had to face, helped me consider every moment as an opportunity to reaffirm my evolving personality. The transformation was so evident that people began to notice; perceiving me more motivated, awake, receptive, and, believe it or not, even funny.

I experienced an unimaginable confidence knowing that, with a strong will, all I yearned for would arrive sooner or later. I learned *to request* without feeling guilty or abusive. Better still, I understood if I did not *wish* and did not create vibration of my aspirations, all the channels through which the results can be obtained would be closed.

The universe kind and immovable waits to be appropriately stimulated, so it will be able to send us the complete repertoire of its beautiful melodies. Like piano keys, only those pressed make sound, and the rest remain silent hoping for the moment our fingers give an impulse to manifest sound.

Thanks to "Radio-Meditation" my mental frequency changed; my "radio station" changed. And I developed the ability to quickly and easily return to my Optimal Point whenever any external aspect threw me to low Decreasing Frequency spaces.

Learning to tune my mind was another of my enormous reforms. But I knew the last step and final touch for a complete recovery was still missing: improving the communication with my internal guide and awakening the Third Original Current... *the Spiritual Energy...*

XII
Our
Spiritual Energy

The Spiritual Energy is the basic current or cosmic channel that offers data with much more elevated vibratory frequencies than those handled by physical and mental matter. And it is also responsible for bringing us higher and altruistic emotions.

In normal conditions, it is not until we turn almost six years old –when our Mental Energy arrives at certain point of frequency– that a *third window* is opened and the Spiritual Current starts to run. This powerful spiritual "blue river" provides us three important aspects:

1- Not just it enables our "Free Will" for making first *moral decisions,* but it urges our mind to reason and question what positive or negative consequences our actions have in ours and others' lives. It makes us more conscious and less instinctive.

2- It sends sensations with stronger frequencies than ones produced by the other two primary energies. These *superior or supreme* emotions are called *values* and facilitate our interaction with the rest of the world. Thus, we have absolute freedom to experience love, respect, compassion, kindness, honesty, loyalty, nobility, strength; or, contrarily, to move away from the central essence and experience hatred, thoughtlessness, selfishness, fear, envy, anger, vanity, vain.

3- And to all privileges we received through the Spiritual Circuit, one more can be added. The opportunity to make contact with the *most valuable* gift evolutionary universal beings may gain: "The Thought Adjuster or Divine Monitor."

The Thought Adjuster arrives in our mind directly from "God" to serve as a mediator between *God and us*. It has the noble objective of boosting our thoughts, improving our life concepts, and clarifying our purpose during the journey to a paradisiacal, perfect, and infinite destiny. This "divine internal voice" that serves as director, guide, or compass, is not just our most-advanced tool, but also comes *individual and exclusive* for each one of us.

With respect and greatness the Thought Adjuster waits patiently to be activated. For then playing the important role to link our personal energy with Creator Energy –as soon as its human partner obtains appropriate mental condition.

Body and *mind* give life to a unique *personality* of each individual. And *personality* together with *spirit* forms the *soul*; special touch that differentiates us from the rest of physical world components.

Our Spiritual Energy at its Optimal Point

Spirit tuning is fundamental element for our passing from an animal instinctive state, or simple physical-mental survival, to another one in which we become more developed and conscious of our real existence as individuals.

When our frequency is raised to Optimal Point we experience this powerful energy that generates a sensation of *beyond*; and although invisible and incomprehensible, it encourages us for continue living and progressing. Contact with this spiritual energy allows us to adopt *values* that fortify our inner self and help us to humanely interact with the rest of the world. *Service* toward others becomes an authentic reason of life, almost a necessity. In addition, we find strength to fight and change what we think is incorrect; promoting right and productive systems for improving society.

Another main aspect of *spiritual* connection is to provide good conditions for which a direct communication between our mind and our "whisperer guide" (*Divine Monitor)* may be established.

This internal *dialogue* adjusts our understanding, and gradually modifies erroneous ideas –acquired through our growth– into *true ones*. It expands our conscience to gain self-knowledge and self-control… to discover an own respectful and valuable character… to find courage for searching progress, success, productivity, and paths of satisfaction.

This spiritual current is a *wise company* offering right words and emotions during confused and hopeless situations; an impulse promoting faith in God, who creates a worthy life for any being choosing to continue the long trip toward *his* divine source.

Let's remember our Mental Energy must flow at a specific volume to generate an appropriate atmosphere in which the spiritual spark may be born. Nevertheless, if the Spiritual Energy is poorly activated or on the contrary over-stimulated, we begin to vibrate in Decreasing or Increasing Spaces and lose all its wonderful benefits.

Our Spiritual Energy in Decreasing Space Levels or Frequential Depression

In same way the other two primary energies manifest in Frequential Spaces and *gradually* build our being, the Spiritual Current does too. Just as Physical and Mental Energies, the Spiritual Current must be constantly stimulated; otherwise, its flow falls into Depressive Frequential Space and all its attributes will be distorted level by level.

And it is level by level –as we go out of tune– we lose sensitivity to the *force of gravity* that attracts us toward central essence of the universe. Doubt and skepticism about existence appears. We don't manage to understand life's real *sense and purpose*. There is an impression something *un-known* is missing, which generates emptiness, loneliness, and hopelessness feelings. So we obsessively lean on others looking for love and support, or we give *divine* attributes to normal flesh-and-bone religious characters who appear more real to our perception.

The less we feel, the less we believe, and our faith crumbles!

Altruistic feelings disappear, one by one; and negative emotions come to life, one by one. It is easy to become prisoners of hatred, jealousy, intolerance, selfishness, greed, and thousands of other low vibrations tormenting and obstructing our soul. Unclear thoughts and emotional instability originates a life full of slips, inadequate behaviors, and sensations far from the ones we wish for. The "Free Will" system begins to fail.

On top of all, when our spiritual foundation is weak, we find great difficulty establishing a relationship with our *Thought Adjuster*; losing its unique, true, and immediate aid. We develop an insecure, skeptical, pessimistic, and incapable of facing life personality. We turn away from the pathway traced and offered by the beautiful universe as our destiny.

Here is one pretty analogy for better understanding. Imagine we are standing in front of a wide, long, well-paved *highway*. It is so extensive that gets lost into horizon and it is impossible to see a finishing point. Next to us, on ground, there is a wooden box that two things can be found when opened: a *letter* and a *small device* similar to a portable radio or walkie-talkie.

The letter reads:

"Hello; welcome to the wonderful world of your own existence. I am the beginning of all creation, although, at the same time, I am the finish line for all evolutionary beings of time and space. I am perfection, fullness, and eternity.

As you may see in your front, there is a pretty road "exclusively" constructed for you that unfolds directly toward my place. If you decide to walk it, I must tell the trajectory is quite extensive, but full of enriching and rewarding elements. Thus, your adventure can begin with certainty that after delighted with the trip you will be at doors for sharing my divine essence.

Observe very carefully what is bordering the even avenue. On each of its sides, two great, dense, and difficult-to-penetrate jungles unfold accompanying the road until the end of its route, as part of the landscape during your voyage.

While keeping your step on the presented path, you are going to experience an incessant diversity of opportunities to construct your personality and develop, more and more, characteristics of perfection. You will have propitious moments to improve all your aptitudes and abilities; obtaining a life full of intention and accomplishment. Dreams will be approachable; triumphs, easy to obtain. In a beauty, harmony, and brightness environment, you will meet beings filled with joy and enthusiasm also eager to walk this trail. And when looking ahead, even so far distance to go, you will know that if continue confidently, someday you will arrive at the final destination.

Your journey will be agile, calm, and comfortable!

Unfortunately, if by own decision or other circumstances, you are pulled toward one shore and go deep into the confusing jungle; the panorama will be very different. You will face a dark, unhealthy, entangled, and difficult-to-pass environment where horizon or noticeable footpaths are no visible. You will have to constantly knock down weeds and bushes to make any progress, and without enough clear spaces that allow you to quicken pace it will always be the same. Dreams will be unapproachable; triumphs, almost impossible to obtain. In addition, you will also find tired, afflicted, lost, and hopeless individuals who do not manage to know for certain a correct direction for leaving this suffocating land.

Your journey will be slow, painful, and exhausting!

Now, observe the other element inside the box. It is an incredible tool of divine spiritual nature and the most valuable gift I can offer you. This device —one highest technology of the universe— has capacity to receive and transmit vibrations, like a small radio-communication device. With it I will be able to hear everything you want to tell me and you will be able to hear everything I have to tell you.

If you yearn for an efficient guide or a voice of support and comfort, just remember your questions will be answered throughout the trip. But there is a single condition: maintain the "little radio" turned on and tuned. Otherwise, at moment your mind lacks contact with this efficient "internal monitor," my message will be lost and you will be alone in your passage.

And no matter whether somebody or a strong wind knocks you down, or if your own adventure desire drags you off track; keep in mind that while the small transistor is working, you will always have the compass and total clarity to retake the beautiful way I specially prepared for you.

I am your destiny. You are the pilot. The Divine Monitor, your copilot. The long avenue, your route. And the surrounding forests, your option.
You decide! "

When our Spiritual Energy is out of tune, we have sensation that we are a loose element without control wandering the universe. When communication with the supreme internal voice is lost, our heart saddens… our soul distorts its essence… and our spirit stops being a spirit.

How can we stimulate our Spiritual Energy and maintain its Optimal Point of Frequency?

The experience of a true and effective Spiritual Current is something has become deformed through time, because we are immersed in cultures with very low self-knowledge and self-development promotion.

Most religions continue preaching retrograde customs and philosophies that go against the real natural way. Limited, old-fashioned, and confusing concepts obstruct progressive ideas flow, therefore many young people (new generations) have moved away from the suitable habit of being in contact with their spiritual side. Do not misinterpret me! I recognize *religion* is a fundamental part of society and can be one of *several* ways for spiritual awakening; but definitely, it must be very well structured and properly handled, otherwise it can create a great barrier between our mind and God.

And even if we decide to be part or not of a religious community, we *yes* must look for environments and activities that allow us to recover our original capacity to connect with the highest source of stimulus - directly received from the divine aid that directs our life.

Let's look some indispensable aspects for tuning our Spiritual Energy:

a) PHYSICAL and MENTAL ENERGY in BALANCE: The first requirement to easily tune the Spiritual Current is to maintain our body and mind in excellent condition.

We already know that if our *mental flow* is far out phase from source, Spiritual Energy is dragged to vibrate in its Decreasing Space. By this, I want to emphasize the importance of working body and mind frequently (as discussed in previous chapters) in order to get a complete intellectual capacity for processing all new and elevated information offered by the Spiritual Current.

b) SELF-COMUNICATION: It is thought that getting in touch with the "inner lantern enlightening the soul" is only for special or chosen people. But we forget this heavenly gift is for all evolutionary beings, or, at least, for those who have a heartfelt wish to take advantage of it.

The practice of speaking with ourselves is an innate instrument from very early age, and this natural instinct continuously urges us to establish an internal interaction. This is why we always are processing daily life happening –either mentally or loudly. For example: "Today I want to organize my time in a better way to accomplished all chores!" "Would my friend be angry if I say the truth?" "The neighbor looks distressed; I am going to see how I can help!"

The intimate *monologue* occurs so easily and mechanically that we neither pay enough attention to it nor realize its whole benefits. There is always something to learn and something to teach with people we share with. But the *chat* with our "I" is what really offers possibility to examine our thoughts without pressure from others; to express our own life's vision fearless of judgment; and to produce suitable vibrations that will catch those exclusive for us universal frequencies.

Reasoning with ourselves helps not only to keep a constant mental energy flowing and to conceptualize everything we experience in an individual manner, but it is the initial step for making contact with our "Thought Adjustor." This process almost always occurs unconsciously and may seem as we are speaking with our own person; however, if we create special conditions, someday we will recognize the *monologue* becomes *dialogue*, distinguishing when our mind is *speaking* and when the Divine Adjuster is.

Now, the best technique to develop efficient self-communication is through a habit many people have been losing in the accelerated and noisy march of present societies: *introspection*.

Having a time of peace and silence, during which we manage to relax and totally concentrate on our existence is *true key* in order to analyze who we are, what we think or feel about everything surrounding us, and which goals we want to achieve. In addition, introspection makes us conscious of changes generated during our personal development.

All this may sound a little complicated, but, really, it is not so difficult and does not require much effort when practiced honestly. Let's look for comfortable, airy, and calm spaces that facilitate an informal "private talk."

Self-communication –in a meditative state– takes us to perceive our thoughts. Identifying our thoughts opens the way for personal discovery. Personal discovery generates a spark that turns the *internal transistor* with which the exciting conversation is settled… conversation that takes our life to a much higher levels.

c) PRAYER: Throughout history, every culture has looked different forms to contact the "creative force." By means of praises, worships, dances, songs, and/or rites, human beings have tried to construct bridges and feel connected with the rest of the cosmos.

Unfortunately *prayer* has also been losing its original structure and, as a result, its effectiveness. Generally, it is loaded with pre-established and unclear concepts that obstruct our true, free, and effective relationship with the Spiritual Energy.

If we want prayer to be fruitful, it must have very particular conditions: First, we have to believe in a superior giver of life energy, with whom fervently we wish to establish a direct bond. Second, mechanically memorized texts that lack logic and sense shouldn't be repeated; rather, we should rationally internalize and visualize the meaning of what is said. And third, prayer must include an internal colloquial environment –even if it is directed toward an external entity such as the Creator, universe, Mother Nature, saints, moon or sun– that allows us to analyze the best way to live life. Where there are questions and answers… where clear and constructive judgments occur… where a calm communication without impositions is opened; like talking with our best friend!

I want to add *group prayer* can be good introduction for individual prayer; however, all the participants must have true common ideals and intentions. Just imagine a meeting where everybody raises energy praying joined hands, and singing accompanied by touching music that increases our "beautiful" voices vibration; effect that connects our spirits on a glad, simple, and mainly natural way.

d) ALTRUISTIC ACTIONS: Desire of giving *love* and purpose of doing *good* towards others are elements that unite us with the great Spiritual Current.

Service is another inevitable requirement for mankind's evolution. In life, sooner or later we face situations that require a productive, honest, and unselfish assistance to others; where we must set aside our own interests for benefit of somebody else.

The results of humanitarian actions increase our spirit's vibration and elevate our being to rejoicing, satisfaction, and fulfillment levels. In the moment we recognize we are pieces of a big social system that must work together to keep the machinery in motion, our essence of kindness and cooperation is activated. However, we must consider the first beneficial work should be done to our own person, and subsequently expanded to others. Loving, respecting, and valuing ourselves sincerely, teaches us to love, respect, and value everybody else in a much more efficient manner.

Now, it is necessary not to confuse *kindness* with *submissiveness*, which frequently occurs because fear, necessity of approval, and lack of security. Pleasing somebody with something that goes against our principles or emotions, simply to avoid being rejected, creates an overall bad feeling and kills the authentic altruistic action sense.

Submission does not elevate the soul; rather, destroys it!

Doing *good* gives us great sense and endless intention of existence. It makes us live sublime emotions and it demonstrates whether our personality is progressing toward the "Divinity" or, contrarily, is moving away from her.

e) *STIMULATING ACTIVITIES:* Frequently many aspects take our energy out of its optimal level of vibration, so we must look for conditions that push our energy back or, better said, to be *re-tuned*.

Conditions that allow us freedom of expression and development… that make our heart beat faster… that offer joy, laughter, and excitement… that take us to feel like floating in clouds, even if just for a little while. Dance and sing at our favorite music band concert or social celebrations; experience new places with exciting cultures; participate in recreational activities or festivals; and enjoy sporting events, where shouting and jumping are allowed. And if desire something more extreme; we may try parachuting out of the sky or canoeing in a turbulent river. However, never underestimate simple things such as getting involved in the peculiar games of the happiest and most extroverted creatures on earth: *children*.

Let's openly enjoy life and express our individuality with respect. Let's feel how our matter vibrates in synchronicity with the universe's force.

Spiritual Energy is the real life giver for our *soul*. This set of a physical body that contains our being, a mind that interprets and analyzes our surroundings, and a spirit, which offers us the possibility of experience consciously living. We must do everything in power to keep the "blue mist" flowing unrestricted, and, at the same time, without excesses; always in balance.

"It is an individual decision to accept or not the Spiritual Energy's help for following our destiny, and we can count on God and the universe highest respect of whatever our choice is. But permitting this supreme current to be part of us, assure an existence of well-being, growth, and eternal evolution. As well as the closure of the whole energy circuit that brings us *totality, integrity, and fulfillment."*

Memories of My Experience...

Many pages would be needed to detail all changes occurred within me when I began to work the Spiritual Energy; and how tuning this current properly was the last piece of the puzzle would help me balance and integrate all components of my being.

Without a doubt, numerous times, I was conscious of the spectacular and *divine* presence that filled my heart with joy and peace; nevertheless, having my body and mind so unbalanced, I felt disconnected and confused. And although I practiced "Radio-Meditation" daily to work out my mind and activated my body three or four times per week, a habit that would generate a good spiritual flow was lacking.

So I engaged in an internal dialogue like when I was a little girl, but this time more efficient and definitely less obsessive than before. And what better way to do it than *transforming* the basic "Radio-Meditation" (list of positive words) into a more personal and intimate prayer.

Evoking the experience when life gave me opportunity to write who I wanted to be and what I wanted to live, I organized a *reflection* for transmitting to God and the rest of the universe who the *new* Patricia was and which frequencies or "radio stations" I wanted to listen to heartily.

The secret was to vibrate with positive desires and *not* with negative memories. Without trying to find solutions for problems or putting limits on when changes should take place; I just had *faith* that creating correct *intentions*, would cause cosmic forces to play their part and generate determinant results. So in a relaxed introspection state, and with hope of opening the window through which the "wind" could enter and move my energies, I daily repeated the following meditation:

"I am pure energy vibrating with the creative central essence. I begin in and finish in it. I am part of the great cosmos that sends God's light to illuminate my body… my mind… my spirit… my heart.

My body is illuminated to live with well-being! Every corner of my physical organism works in rhythm and coordination; offering me health, comfort, and freedom of movement. I feel full of energy and vitality. There is beauty, balance, and excellence.

My mind is illuminated, having clarity of existence! I understand who I am, where I come from, and where I will go. I have an intellect able to listen to the internal voice that guides my steps. I am wisdom in what I think, what I speak, and what I do; security in my decisions and certainty of taking the correct roads that bring self-knowledge and accomplishments; creativity to obtain efficiency in my home, work, and social performance. There is clarity and truth.

My spirit is illuminated and grows consciousness! I feel the universe's vigor giving me courage to face any obstacle with calm, tranquility, and success. I have confidence every day occurs in suitable way and conviction that I am owner, creator, and artisan of my destiny... of my present... of my future. There is strength and integrity.

My heart is illuminated to experience the true pleasure of life! I offer and receive love, continuously. Joy, laughter, and humor are part of my habits. I exhibit kindness, cordiality, and sincerity with others. I pardon those who have hurt me. I free myself from situations blocking my connection with the primary energies. There is tranquility and peace.

I thank God and all connected universal forces for offering me growth, evolution, prosperity, and abundance; allowing me to flow in the beautiful river of the divine current."

For closing, I did a little talk with myself. Recalling what I had done during the day, visualizing my wishes for the following day, and then leaving my mind blank for few minutes.

Thus, ready to have sweet dreams, I retired to my bedroom!

I never thought this simple and short *meditation*, consciously done, could be such an effective tool.

Many new and convenient concepts arrived to me. My security and independence were improving. The route of my destiny began to appear urging me to follow it. The desire to share my history, helping others, and giving back to God took an unexpected force and eased my transformation.

For first time, I perceived myself *complete*. With physical well-being; with a calm, clear, and optimistic mind; with a proud and brave spirit able to change situations that I didn't like; and, best of all, with a favorable environment in which my evolution may continue.

I had forgotten what *wishing* and *executing* attitudes were like, but I found the opportunity for vindication. I put together a "creative dance" program for children, started to give inspirational talks and workshops, and then embraced the great adventure of writing this book.

The most impressive ability I acquired was facing things calmly; holding a correct attitude while enjoying the journey without being frustrated about not arriving immediately to the destination. I was pleased not only with victory, but also with the process of obtaining it; living minute by minute with required emotion and intensity.

I must confess it felt very strange! Me waking up in the morning and feeling anguish free, with many plans to accomplish, facing daily ups and downs with good attitude, creating solutions, and being grateful for existence.

It was hard to believe the shy and inexpressive girl from the past was now stepping in front of groups of people, speaking and encouraging them to live and attain their own dreams. Remembering that we all are important beings with innate capacities to move forward... that Depression is not a disease of which we are victims, but rather a condition can be overcome naturally and effectively… that the "mighty one" powerful energy flows constantly whenever we are in tune.

On numerous occasions, submerged in a confused reality, I wanted to change my whole life; *be able to go away from this planet*. Luckily, today I understand the contact with the Spiritual Energy assured me to keep a correct pathway. That in the future when I have to leave this world, I will be satisfied for having used the complete repertoire of tools my internal nature offers. And whether I obtained many or few results, what matters is my commitment and determination for being better; for feeling closer to The Creator's perfect essence; and for finishing someday this exciting voyage, regardless of how much time it will take…

XIII
Overcoming Depression

All Depression symptoms may be eradicated not only when each essential energy (Physical, Mental, or Spiritual) recovers the Optimal Point of its original frequency, but also when all three currents flow in line or alignment.

Let's use a stereophonic *radio* as an example. Its *equalizer* board is formed by three horizontal bars, parallel to each other, which control different components of sound. Let's say the first bar reproduces the sounds of instruments with low pitches; the second row amplifies instruments of medium pitches; and the third one, high pitches.

Every canal has an interior small button that adjusts side to side, depending on what we want to highlight while listening the transmission. The sound is perceived progressively weaker if the button moves leftward away from *midpoint*; and the sound is progressively stronger if it moves rightward away from *midpoint*. (See graphic No. 10).

Equalizer is used to adjust reproduction frequencies of a range of sounds, with the purpose of matching its original emission. Better said, to manipulate different music tones and be played in a balanced, harmonious way.

The three buttons can be moved randomly and unlimited combinations of the same musical piece are obtained. With an *imbalanced or unaligned* board configuration the instruments and voices of the singers are lost, or perhaps some sounds are highly accentuated overshadowing the rest.

Graphic No. 10

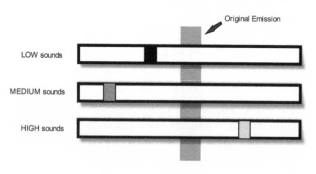

MISALIGNMENT, DESYNCHRONIZATION, IMBALANCE

Original Emission

LOW sounds

MEDIUM sounds

HIGH sounds

But if the three knobs are *balanced or aligned* – positioned exactly one underneath the other, forming a straight line down the middle of the board– each musical part manifests its best, and sound is perceived clear, complete, clean, and pleasant. (See graphic No. 11)

Graphic No. 11

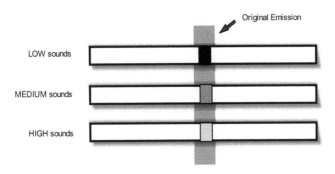

ALIGNMENT, SYNCHRONIZATION, BALANCE

Now, as radio universal vibration amplifiers, we also have a *natural equalizer*, and each one of the primary energies (Physical, Mental, and Spiritual) may move independently in its own canal or Frequential Space. This way our personality changes depending on where every frequency of the *tricolor melody* is placed.

When the three currents are in *alignment* or *synchronization* we assure a vivacious-easy-flowing stream of essential raw material, and our character manifests stable. In contrast, when the currents are in *misalignment or desynchronization* (one, two, or three of the currents go from midpoint frequency to either Decreasing or Increasing Space levels) our vital flow is affected in different ways. (See graphic No. 12)

Graphic No. 12

RED Energy

YELLOW Energy

BLUE Energy

If we create the habit of indiscriminately altering the frequencies of our energies, we exhibit destabilized personalities. A positive situation quickly becomes negative; a depressive state rises to a stressful one; or euphoria diminishes to sadness.

And although it is impossible to deny that human nature is variable, changeable, and movable; it should never fall into *unstable*, because having a bad time and feeling sad about something that marks our emotions is very different from being *prisoners* of unceasing mood changes.

Let's see another condition!

When just some of the primary energies are balanced and the rest are forced to remain out of tune. This generates individuals who are successful in some aspects of life, but mistaken in others. For example, those who keep active and healthy body, however, they are emotionally unfortunate. Or those who are excellent at work, but their body keep sick and their spirit holds great emptiness. Or perhaps those who present a kind spiritual identity, but their performance in work and social environments is difficult.

The most critical part is when the three currents are pushed to vibrate *together* and *constantly* in any Frequential Space, creating chronic *Depression or Stress* circumstances. In this permanent imbalance, no life's facet works and can take the person to limits of desperation, collapse, and even self-destruction.

Point of Balance Displacement

Vibrating just for a while far from Optimal Point is not a problem, because naturally and instinctively our energy returns to its initial place of balance. Physical, Mental, and Spiritual energies were perfectly designed for self-regulation, always searching to go back to a harmonic state whenever some temporarily stimulus removes them from their balance –like a pendulum moving side to side after being pushed, but inevitably looks to return to the center of its axis.

The problem is created when the three primary energies hold misplaced, persists at some Decreasing Space level, and the axis of balance moves toward lower steps of its original frequency. Usually our bad habits and inadequate external circumstances *force* our frequencies to vibrate out of tune. Creating a *false zone* of balance where our energies look to return – actually are *forced* to return– not to Optimal Point, but to a lower vibratory level that becomes their resting "temporary home." (See graphic No. 13) Thus, Depression becomes normal and chronic!

Graphic No. 13

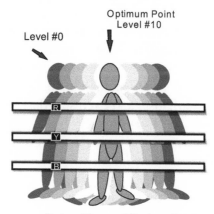

False Zone of Balance

For better understanding let me say: if my habitual disposition is *happiness* (level 10), and a heated discussion with my son knocks me down to lower levels like 5 or 4, uncomfortable and negative sensations are generated. But I can be sure sooner or later *inertia* makes me recover the initial emotion of happiness, because my vibrations go up again to true balance at level 10… because that is my *normal* point of vibration.

It would be very different if my *everyday* energy states at level 4. This time the same fight with my son knocks me down to steps much lower (such as level 1 or 0) where negative sensations are manifested in a difficult to bear intensity; and although I try to be calm, my sadness doesn't return to the joy offered by level 10, and instead it is forced to go back to conditions expressed by level 4.

Perhaps my energy is used to vibrate at level 3 that generates a condition of pain, irritability, distress, and passivity. But if I have a positive motivation, such as my dearest friend visit, my vibrations raise several points (let's say to level 8) and momentarily my body feels more vigor, the sadness dissipates a little, and I almost experience joy.

Now, what happens when my friend is gone? The positive impulse ends. Again my energies seek the usual level in which they vibrate. In this case it is number 3 that makes me experience, once more, the disagreeable properties associated with such a low position, and not the *natural* joy from level 10.

Happiness stops being a permanent manifestation and becomes something sporadic!

This is why commonly depressive people feel small problems greater and more devastating than they really are. It also explains why when we open our eyes in the morning we continue feeling bad without apparent reason, since overnight the body decreases its frequency greatly, and when waking up our vibrations don't return to high levels, but continue being *stuck* in some Decreasing Space position.

No matter how many good things surround us, sooner or later our bodies, thoughts, and emotions are compelled to return to out of tune frequencies when the balance point is misplaced. So it is necessary to find ways of *reprogramming* ourselves and getting into the habit of being connected with "original stations."

Reprogramming

When we want to listen to a new radio station, the dial has to be moved toward new radial frequency; and if we want to hear clear and harmonic sound, the equalizer buttons have to be kept in correct position.

This way, the radio is ready to play our favorite music every time it is turned on.

Reprogramming ourselves means not only recovering the original frequency of each one of our three essential currents, but *keeping* them aligned in the same tuned zone. For an effective reprograming, several aspects have to be considered:

- Choose appropriate activities that stimulate our body, our mind, and our spirit individually (see previous chapters); never forgetting they have to give us pleasure.

- The selected activities must be done periodically in order to acquire stable habits. The ideal time is about ten or fifteen minutes daily; if every day basis becomes difficult, try at least three or four times per week, in periods of twenty-five minutes to an hour.

- Each current can be neither too little stimulated nor too much stimulated, just maintained in an average term that assures frequencies analogous to universal circuits. The "thermometer" that indicates if we are in the right level of stimulation is the *positive* sensation we get after each current is activated and how long this satisfaction lasts during the day. So any *negative* feeling is warning sign that we are under or over the right frequency point.

- Be open for personal transformations, aware of attitude changes in people around, and ready to take advantage of new roads and opportunities offered by the universe.

Whether we decide to dance, swim, take up a sport, or have a pleasant long walk by the park; the fundamental element to stimulate our body is to wake up each corner of it through movement and appropriate breathing. Complement this with moderate sun exposure, more healthy-balanced diet, and natural-airy-clean environments.

To keep our mind in shape, *meditation* grants the ability to replace negative thoughts with positives ones, and hold an enthusiastic and optimistic life conceptualization. We may reinforce our mental skills using logic and mathematic disciplines.

And for our spirit, as a final touch, we may pray or establish a pleasant conversation with our inner voice through peaceful self-gathering moments; supported with any other pleasant dynamic that allows us freedom of expression.

To diminish erroneous habits that force our energies to vibrate in low frequencies, we must adopt routines that match the complete universal positive frequencies spectrum; assuring the correct flow of sensations, thoughts, emotions, and conditions required for our development.

"Tuning and reprogramming ourselves are the best means to face Depression... the true means to overcome this condition that disable our existence."

Conclusion of My Experience...

Looking back, everything seems like a distressing dream from which I have fortunately awoken. Depression appears as a condition that was never part of me; and the anxiety veil has been exchanged for energy of well-being, balance, fullness, and security.

It is hard to imagine three basic aspects as *movement, Radio-Meditation, and introspection* today are the base that supports my existence structure; allowing my boat to keep afloat and remain in alignment with the river of energy arranged long time ago as my destiny.

Luckily, I understand now although my life has been transformed in a miraculous way, it will never stop changing. Because I am convinced that disadvantages and difficulties are going to continue taking place; that many times I will trip over bitter people, incapable of offering something positive; that society will hold absurd, violent, and destructive situations; and the thick jungles bordering my pathway, will remain there forever. But knowing the power to counteract this reality is in my hands provides me tranquility. And whenever, for any reason, my energies leave their optimal frequency, it won't be necessary to blame others or feel like a victim, but rather *practical measures* can be taken for carrying on.

This sounds unbelievable! The girl, who one day thought everything was finished for her and would never escape such a miserable situation, today is proving the opposite. Showing that, yes, it can be done. Reaffirming that transformation occurs depending of intensity of our desires and mental vibrations. That producing great changes in our own personality is the first step to obtaining beneficial reforms in our surroundings, and the decision to be guided by the internal voice will ensure us to stay on a paved road and attain gifts from infinite. And it doesn't matter what difficult or traumatic situations push us to vibrate at low frequencies, if with true feeling of our heart, we yearn to return to the essential departure point, the universe will be our awakening promoter and accomplice for retaking our celestial path.

Depression is a group of negative symptoms formed by our incapacity for connecting with the *omnipotent source,* and occurs when natural windows through which universal circuits flow within us are closed. It is a position out of tune and full of interference. However, creation is so extraordinary. It gives us the possibility to come to this world loaded with simple, practical, pleasant, and completely natural tools, which can be used to get a free flow of our essential energies and to invade our beings with their powerful vigor.

We are a set of a physical body that contains our self and allows us to experience time and space; a mental system that processes all cosmic information, helping us to form own concepts about existence; and a heart feeling exciting emotions, that incites us to follow the route toward the powerful force that gave us birth. Never forgetting our only responsibility since the day we are born is to maintain the energetic trio at exact frequency. While vibrating aligned and synchronized, the connection with *truth* is unbroken and we can avoid living with distortions, illusions, mirages, and falsehoods.

And if these words sound like those of a dreamer or idealistic person, I would say it is completely opposite. Because a system as huge and magnificently designed as the cosmos was not created for us to live in pain, bitterness, and sorrow; really, it was conceived for us to be crossed with enthusiasm and pleasure.

Many years have passed. Yes! Many years of experience. A magical childhood. A difficult awakening. An inexplicable encounter with energies and emotions. A sea of sadness. And many times a consciousness out of reality. But, there were also times of great changes. Deep desires. New strategies. Self-discovery and self-control. Illumination and understanding. Offering and receiving disposition. And mainly, a world of adventure.

I always thank God for giving me the opportunity to become an *"Ex-depressive."* For bringing me comprehension that the universe is not scarce, it doesn't die, it just continues eternally vibrating. And it never gives up on us… although we give up on it.

But, at the moment of firm desire, we will be able to feel again its powerful energy!

Farewell

****

If today you want to think everything makes sense; your life and the existence of all universal elements have value and a particular intention.

If, finally, you wish to leave the treacherous currents drowning you, and move into a firm and secure land that allows you to freely breathe and opens the door for a calm, pleasant, and exciting path.

If you yearn for the energy to recover the place where it belongs, for motivation being reborn, for joy and humor to perform their duty, and for the cinematographic tape of your existential film leaves the pause and continues rolling.

If your true desire is returning to be happy; you have just taken the first step in making a great change, for which I heartily congratulate you. Keep going forward and never doubt, even for a second, that as well as I managed to overcome Depression... you are going to do it too.

Good luck and never forget *"If the raw material with which the universe has been created is love, balance, wisdom, abundance, joy, and perfection. And you are part of the universe, not more important that a sand grain, but no less valuable than your own creator; then, how can you doubt 'you' also are love, balance, wisdom, abundance, joy, and perfection?"*

Your Opinion Is Very Important
****

If you enjoyed this book and it has been a good pathway for growing personally, I would love to hear from you.

Your opinion is very important because it will help other people identify how this book may help them.

Please write your *constructive comment* on "Amazon" website, where all my books can be found in kindle and paperback:

www.amazon.com/author/patriciagaviria

Thank you so much for your support!!

About the Author
Patricia Gaviria
****

*Author, Practitioner & Coach of Holistic Wellness.

*Amazon Best-Selling Author with her books in English, Spanish, and Portuguese.
*Recognized by The International Latino Book Award 2015 in United States.
*Creator & Practitioner of Radio-Meditation, Natural Tuning, and Cards of Wisdom.
*Accredited by life experience, especially in the subject of Depression.
*Emissary of her Postulate "Bio-Antenna Effect"

From a young age, Patricia has used the help of her Thought Adjuster not only to understand life with broader concepts but also to generate positive and transforming personal changes. In 2004, she founded the movement "Moving Energies" to help integral social development through inspirational talks, workshops, advice, and classes.

Other of her books in English>
-Tuning Our Physical, Mental, and Spiritual Energies Naturally: Bio-Antenna Effect
-Latest in Divine Technology: The Thought Adjusters
-Recovering my Body, my Mind, and my Spirit

in Spanish>

-Volver a Ser Feliz... Venciendo la Depresión con el Cuerpo, la Mente y el Espíritu (original title)
-Efecto Radio-Antena... Sintonizando Nuestras Energías Física, Mental y Espiritual
-Lo Último en Tecnología Divina: Los Ajustadores de Pensamiento
-Recuperando mi Cuerpo, mi Mente y mi Espíritu

in Portuguese>

-Voltar a Ser Feliz... Vencendo a Depressão com o Corpo, a Mente e o Espírito

For More Information:

www.amazon.com /author/patriciagaviria
www.gaviriapatricia.blogspot.com

Moving Energies

Milton Keynes UK
Ingram Content Group UK Ltd.
UKHW011318091123
432266UK00004B/424